MEN
WHO MISSED IT

CHARLES EVANS HUGHES

MEN
WHO MISSED IT

Great Americans Who
Missed the White House

By

Clarence Edward Noble Macartney, 1879-1957

Illustrated

Essay Index Reprint Series

BOOKS FOR LIBRARIES PRESS
FREEPORT, NEW YORK

First Published 1940
Reprinted 1970

INTERNATIONAL STANDARD BOOK NUMBER:
0-8369-1835-5

LIBRARY OF CONGRESS CATALOG CARD NUMBER:
76-128274

PRINTED IN THE UNITED STATES OF AMERICA

FOREWORD

MEN WHO MISSED IT

There is a tradition that Stephen A. Douglas, Lincoln's opponent in the election of 1860, exclaimed on his deathbed, with his last breath, "I missed it!" Was he thinking of the presidency which had eluded his grasp?

The men who aspired to the presidency, but missed it, are, as a group, much more distinguished, able and illustrious than those who achieved it. There are no ten presidents who can match for ability, brilliancy of mind, and for public service ten such men as Clay, Seward, Webster, Calhoun, Chase, Greeley, McClellan, Blaine, Bryan, and La Follette.

Why is it that so often in our political history the ablest and strongest men failed to attain unto the presidency, whereas, in not a few instances, mediocre men, who were not worthy to unloose the shoe lachets of these other men, were elected president? There were many factors which entered into the defeat of the great men, like those named above, who sought after the presidency, but never saw their ambition fulfilled. One reason was that men of great ability arouse jealousies by reason of their great ability. In the game of politics, too, political managers have often found it to their interest to select comparatively unknown candidates who have never expressed themselves on public issues, and therefore have not aroused antagonism. Men like Chase and Seward, who had been so outspoken on the slavery question, were passed by for a man like Lincoln, who, in comparison with them, had been careful and cautious in his utterances.

Personal feuds and enmities, too, played an important part. Greeley's resentment of his treatment at the hand of Seward twenty years before made him an active opponent of Seward at the Convention of 1860. Conkling's undying resentment of the ridicule Blaine once heaped upon him in Congress was the real secret of Blaine's defeat in 1884. An unwise letter, too, or utterance, on the part of the candidate has compassed his defeat, such as the letter Clay wrote in the campaign of 1844 on the admission of Texas. Errors of judgment, too, on the part of political managers have defeated able candidates. A striking instance of this was the defeat of Hughes when he lost California. Distinguished men, such as Webster, never reached the goal of their ambition because they had no strong political organization back of them.

The story of the great men who aspired to the presidency but missed it is full of human interest, sometimes of sorrow and tragedy.

CONTENTS

ILLUSTRATIONS

"But, sir," he added, "it is a great office. Why, Mr. Bates, it is the greatest office in the world, and I am but a man, sir. I want it! I want it!"

—*Daniel Webster, after his defeat for the nomination at the Whig Convention, 1852.*

I

AARON BURR

Aaron Burr might have been president of the United States if he had had more moral character. It is true that men with serious blemishes on their character were elevated to the presidency. Andrew Jackson was stained with the blood of his fellowman, slain in a duel. Another president in the midst of a heated campaign acknowledged the paternity of an illegitimate child. These were particular acts and faults which the public overlooked and forgot. But with Aaron Burr it was different. The whole tone of his life was low. He was of the earth, earthy. Men did not trust him, and it was that that cost him the presidency.

Had Burr succeeded in his presidential ambitions, he would have been the ablest man, intellectually, ever to have occupied that highest office in the whole world. No man inherited more. His father was Aaron Burr, Presbyterian clergyman, and second president of Princeton College, and his grandfather America's greatest thinker, Jonathan Edwards, author of the celebrated treatise on the "Will," and third president of Princeton.

Born at Newark, New Jersey, February 6, 1756, Burr graduated at Princeton at the age of sixteen. At Princeton there remain two traditions of his licentiousness and unbelief. One, that during the Whitefield revivals which shook the college, Burr shut himself up in his room, telling his college mates that he would settle the matter of belief or unbelief that night. Late at

9

night, students passing under his windows heard the shutters suddenly thrown wide, and Burr's voice rang out, "'Goodbye, God!'" The other tradition is a lonely grave on the campus, said to be the grave of a Princeton girl who was seduced by Burr, and who when dying requested to be buried at the spot where he had accomplished her ruin.

In the Revolutionary War Burr served with gallantry as a staff officer in the unfortunate expedition to Quebec and took part in the battles of Long Island and Monmouth. He was for a time on Washington's staff, also, and left so unfavorable an impression of himself that when Madison and Monroe asked Washington when he was president to name Burr as Minister to France, Washington declined to do so, saying that he made it a rule never to appoint to a high post a man of whose integrity he was not assured.

Burr resigned from the Army in 1779, was admitted to the bar in New York in 1782, and in 1783 married in the little brownstone church at Paramus, New Jersey, the beautiful and charming Theodosia Prevost, widow of a British officer. At New York Burr quickly established himself as one of the two leading lawyers of the city. The other was Alexander Hamilton. He at once engaged in the politics of the state, was elected its attorney-general, and in 1791 entered the United States Senate. Burr was admired and supported by a group of young men whom he had captivated and who were known as the "Little Band." In his campaigns Burr was the first to make use of the Tammany Society as a political agency.

As early as 1797, when John Adams was elected president, Burr received thirty electoral votes. In 1800 the Democrats, or Republicans, as they were then

AARON BURR

known, put Jefferson and Burr at the head of their ticket. At that time electors voted only for president, and the second highest in the electoral college became vice-president. It was generally understood, however, in 1800 that Jefferson was the candidate for the presidency. Burr managed to manipulate elections in some of the states so that he and Jefferson each received 73 votes in the electoral college. This threw the election into the House of Representatives, where the Federalists held the balance of power. For 35 ballots Jefferson and Burr were deadlocked. On the thirty-sixth ballot Jefferson was chosen president and Burr became vice-president.

Had Burr come out and manfully declared that Jefferson was the one whom the Democrat-Republicans had put up for the presidency, undoubtedly he could have become president at a subsequent election. But his conspiracy to steal the election from Jefferson discredited him with honorable men everywhere and forfeited him the confidence and support of his own party.

After the Burr-Jefferson contest, the necessity for a change in the Constitution governing the election of the vice-president was recognized by the country, and in a period of ten months the Constitutional Amendment was adopted which requires electors to vote separately for President and Vice-President.

One of the determining factors in the defeat of Burr in the House of Representatives was the influence of Alexander Hamilton with the Federalists. Hamilton took an active part in opposition to Burr, and in his letters and conversations attacked his character. In a letter to one, Wolcott, he wrote: "These things are to be inferred with moral certainty from the character of the man. Every step in his career proves that he has formed himself upon the model of Catiline." In a letter to Bayard of Delaware, who played an important part in the election of Jefferson, Hamilton wrote: "Let me add that I could scarcely name a discreet man of either party in our state who does not think Mr. Burr the most unfit man in the United States for the office of president. Disgrace abroad, ruin at home, are the probable fruits of his elevation."

In 1804 Burr sought to retrieve his political fortunes by running for the governorship of New York. He was defeated; and again it was Hamilton who played a large part in his defeat. During the campaign there appeared letters in the newspapers in which Hamilton was represented to have said that Burr was a "dangerous man, and one that ought not to be trusted with the reins of government." To this was added the statement that there was "a still more despicable opinion which General Hamilton had expressed of Mr. Burr."

Stung and embittered by this second defeat, and by the part Hamilton had played in it, Burr demanded of Hamilton an avowal or a disavowal of the statements which had appeared in the press. Hamilton quibbled and evaded, and Burr then called him out. The fatal duel on the "tragic shores of Weehawken" then followed, July 11, 1804. This duel was the end of Burr as a national figure. Then came his grandiose scheme in the southwest for some kind of plot against Spain and the establishment of a trans-Mississippi empire. Burr was tried for treason before John Marshall at Richmond and was acquitted, despite the eloquent arraignment of the great orator, William Wirt, whose description of Burr entering Blennerhasset Island as the serpent entered Eden has become an American classic.

After years of wandering abroad, and vain attempts to interest England and Napoleon in his Mexican conspiracy, Burr returned in 1812 to the United States, where he re-established himself in his practice as a lawyer. He died in loneliness and poverty in 1836. Thwarted and disappointed in his political ambitions, the great joy, and the great tragedy, too, of Burr's life, was his gifted and beautiful daughter, Theodosia, wife of James Alston, the governor of South Carolina. Burr adored this daughter and was adored by her in return. In a letter to her father Theodosia wrote that only religious reverence kept her from worshiping him as a god.

On a December day in 1812 she set sail on a packet ship at Georgetown, South Carolina, to visit her father at New York. The ship was never heard of again. During the last years of Burr's life, frequenters of the Battery at New York would see a bent old man walk down to the water front, and putting his hand to shade his eyes, gaze earnestly down the harbor towards the sea, looking in vain for the ship which never arrived.

II

HENRY CLAY

If Henry Clay had not written an unwise letter during the campaign of 1844, he would have been elected president.

No man in the history of the country ever had such a popular following as Henry Clay. Senator August H. Shepherd, of North Carolina, once remarked of Clay: "He can get more people to run after him and hear him speak, and fewer to vote for him, than any other man in America." The son of a Baptist minister, Clay was born April 12, 1777, in Hanover County, Virginia, the county that gave two other great Americans to the nation, Patrick Henry, and the greatest of the colonial preachers, Samuel Davies, and one of Princeton's presidents. After a brief schooling and some experience as clerk of the Chancery Court at Richmond, Clay followed the "Go West, young man" movement of his day and settled in Kentucky, where he quickly established his fame as a criminal lawyer.

Clay entered the Senate in 1809 to fill out an unexpired term, but after a year resigned and was elected to the House. The purpose of the change was that he might get closer to the people. In the difficulties that arose with England, Clay was strongly anti-British and pro-war and boasted that if war came the Kentucky Militia could take Canada unaided. When the War of 1812 came to an end he was one of the American commissioners who signed the Treaty of Ghent. By this time Clay's influence in Kentucky was supreme, and he was famed throughout the nation as an advocate of the "American System," which meant protective tariff and internal improvements. He was a chief proponent of the National Pike, or Cumberland Road, now Highway 40, the great road that first united the East with the West, and was to the country what the transcontinental railroads are now.

Clay's first try for the presidency was in 1824, when he ran against Andrew Jackson, John Quincy Adams, and William H. Crawford of Georgia. He received the lowest vote of the four and was eliminated from the names to be voted on in the House of Representatives, into which the election was thrown because none of the candidates had received a majority. Jackson had a plurality, and the Kentucky Legislature instructed Clay to cast his vote for Jackson. Clay obeyed these instructions by working and voting in the House for Adams, who was elected. Adams made Clay the Secretary of State, a post which he filled with great distinction. He was an ardent advocate of the independence of the South American republics, where he was regarded as a popular hero.

Clay's support of Adams against Jackson, and his presence in the cabinet of Adams, made him the object of bitter attack by his former associates, who charged him with having entered into a deal with Adams. Eccentric and brilliant John Randolph of Virginia rose in the Senate on March 27, 1826, and pilloried Clay and Adams for corruption. In this mad phillipic Randolph likened Clay and Adams to Judas Iscariot, and then said, "I was defeated horsefoot and dragoons ——— cut up ——— and clean broke down ——— by the coalition of Bliffil and Black George ——— by the combination, unheard of till then, of the Puritan with the Blackleg."

Enraged by this insult, Clay, who had already fought one duel, sent a challenge to Randolph. When they met on a Virginia hillside both men fired and missed. At the second discharge Clay's bullet pierced Randolph's gown, but Randolph fired into the air, exclaiming as he did so, "I do not fire at you, Mr. Clay." When Clay expressed his joy that Randolph had not been hurt, the latter remarked, "You owe me a coat, Mr. Clay." Clay answered, "I am glad the debt is no greater," and with that the duel ended and they returned to Washington.

John Quincy Adams, the successful candidate in 1824, described himself as a man of reserve, cold, austere, and forbidding in manners, in whom his political adversaries saw a gloomy misanthrope and his personal enemies an unsocial savage. With a view to popularizing Adams in the campaign, and, if possible, dispel rumors about his cold, austere personality, some of his political backers persuaded him to attend a cattle show at Worcester, Massachusetts, so that he might mingle with the common people. As he was going about viewing the exhibits, a farmer came up to him and said:

"Mr. Adams, I am very glad to see you. My wife when she was a gal lived in your father's family. You were then a little boy, and she has told me a great deal about you. She very often combed your head."

"Well," said Mr. Adams, in his harsh way, "I suppose she combs yours now."

Whereupon the discomfited farmer retreated in chagrin and Adams had lost one more vote.

Adams felt that Webster's friendship for Clay was "false, insidious, and treacherous," and that from the "day I quitted the walls of Harvard, Henry Clay, Wil-

HENRY CLAY

liam H. Crawford, John C. Calhoun, Andrew Jackson, Daniel Webster and John Randolph have used up their faculties in base and dirty tricks to thwart my progress in life and destroy my character."

A powerful but tragic personality in the four-cornered race for the presidency in 1824 was William H. Crawford of Georgia. Born in Virginia, Crawford had been brought up in Columbia County, Georgia. He had the advantage of studying at Carmel Academy under the great schoolmaster, Moses Waddell, son of James Waddell, the famous blind preacher of Virginia, immortalized by William Wirt in his eloquent description of a sacramental sermon he heard Waddell preach in which the preacher said, "Socrates died like a philosopher, but Jesus Christ died like a god."

Gigantic in stature, handsome of face, and engaging in person, Crawford quickly became a power in politics in Georgia, and in 1807 was elected to the United States Senate. By this time, like many of his political contemporaries, Crawford had engaged in several bloody duels. In 1802 he killed Peter L. Van Allen, and in 1806 was dangerously wounded himself by General John Clark. Crawford was made president *pro tempore* of the Senate upon the death of Vice-President Clinton, and in 1813 was appointed by Madison as minister to France. After that he became Secretary of War under Madison, and then Secretary of the Treasury. Many of the Democrat-Republicans favored him as the next president rather than Monroe. But Crawford stood aside for Monroe, and served as Secretary of the Treasury in both of the Monroe administrations.

When the campaign of 1824 opened, Crawford received nearly all of the votes of the Democratic caucus in the House of Representatives. Albert Gallatin was named for the vice-presidency, but withdrew in October because of the outcry against him on the ground that he was not a native of the United States. In the popular vote for president, Adams had 84 electoral votes, Jackson 97, Crawford 41, and Clay 37. In the midst of the campaign Crawford's majestic body was stricken with paralysis, and for a time he lay unable to speak or see. He never fully recovered the vigor of his body or mind. He became a judge in Georgia, and died in 1834, leaving the political arena to his great adversaries and contemporaries, Jackson, Clay, and Calhoun. He cherished a hopeless ambition for the White House until death ended his career.

Frustrated in his own ambitions for the presidency, Crawford played a prominent part in frustrating the presidential ambitions of John C. Calhoun. He let it be known in letter and by conversation that it had been Calhoun, and not he, who had proposed at a cabinet meeting in 1818 that Andrew Jackson be court martialed for having invaded the Spanish territory of Florida. This helped to bring about the break between Jackson and Calhoun, and put an end to the presidential ambitions of the great South Carolinian. In the correspondence which ensued between Crawford and Calhoun, Crawford denounced Calhoun as a "corrupt, degraded, and disgraced man, for whom no man of honor and character could feel any other than the most sovereign contempt."

In 1832 Clay was nominated by the anti-Jackson men, but was badly defeated by Jackson in the election. But by 1840 the country had had enough of Jackson and Van Buren, and almost anybody the Whigs nominated was likely to be elected. Clay thought that his time had come; but the convention passed him over and nominated a military nobody, William H. Harrison, who was elected in the famous "Log Cabin and Hard Cider," "Tippecanoe and Tyler too" campaign.

The power behind the scenes in the 1839 convention was the New York politician, Thurlow Weed, of the political firm of "Weed, Seward, and Greeley." Weed felt that the Whigs had a better chance to elect a nobody like Harrison than a popular idol like Clay. But after nominating Harrison, the convention, somewhat frightened and abashed at what they had done, spent an hour or more eulogizing Clay, with statements to the effect that he had so much honor and prestige in the country that the presidency could add little to it.

At this convention, held in a Lutheran church in Harrisburg, Dec. 4, 1839, John Tyler of Virginia was so overcome with grief at Harrison's nomination and Clay's defeat that he shed copious tears. The convention finally named Tyler as a running mate for Harrison, with the hope that putting so warm a friend of Clay on the ticket would do much to placate the aggrieved followers of Clay.

But that did not go down with Clay. When Wise of Virginia brought the news of what the convention had done to Clay at his boarding house at Washington, Clay exclaimed, "Damn them! Damn them! I knew it! I knew it! My friends are not worth the powder it would take to blow them up." Then, shaking his fist at Wise, Clay said, "If there were two Henry Clays, one of them would make the other president of the United States. I am always run by my friends when sure to be defeated, and now betrayed for a nonentity when I, or anyone, would be sure to be elected."

In 1844 the Whig Convention nominated him by acclamation. Polk was the Democratic candidate and the issue of the campaign was the admission of Texas and the expansion of slavery. Clay tried to sidestep this issue, and took the position that the question of slavery was not involved in the matter of the annexation ot Texas. To the editor of an Alabama paper he wrote that he had no personal objection to the annexation, but that he would be unwilling to see the Union dissolved or seriously jeopardized for the sake of acquiring Texas. He declared that the paramount object of his public life was the preservation of the Union. He would be glad to see Texas annexed if it could be done without dishonor or war, with the common consent of the Union, and upon just and fair terms. He could not see that the question of Texas was affected by slavery one way or the other, for that institution was destined to become extinct at some distant day "by the operation of the inevitable laws of population."

This letter lost Clay the election. Birney, the Abolition candidate, received 15,000 votes in New York. These votes, most of them taken from former Clay supporters, lost Clay New York and the election. Once, when warned that a proposed statement on the slavery question might lose him anti-slavery votes, Clay answered with his memorable utterance, "I would rather be right than president." But it was the lack of a firm and courageous stand on the matter of Texas that lost him the election of 1844.

The campaign was one of great bitterness. Clay was attacked as a dueler, Sabbath breaker, gambler and murderer. A Democratic campaign pamphlet ran the following in bold type:

"CHRISTIAN VOTERS!
READ, PAUSE, AND REFLECT
MR. CLAY'S
MORAL CHARARCTER!

A Democratic member of the House said that Clay's standard should consist of his armorial bearing, and that these ought to be a pistol, a pack of cards, and a brandy bottle. Clay got word of his defeat when he was attending a wedding at Lexington. A friend handed him a paper. When he opened it and read the death knell of his lifelong ambition, a blue shadow passed slowly over his face, and he stood for a moment motionless. Then he laid down the paper, and turning to a table, filled a glass with wine, and raising it to his lips, said, "I drink to the health and happiness of all assembled here."

The defeat of Clay stunned the nation. Never in the history of the country did a political defeat bring such sorrow and lamentation to the better classes of American society. Clay courageously drank his cup of bitter disappointment, and other cups, too, of bitter personal grief, for one son was in an insane asylum and another died in the Mexican War. The last years of his life were devoted to a noble effort to preserve the Union by political compromise. He died at Washington, June 29, 1851, and the nation which had repeatedly refused to elevate him to the presidency now paused to pay the dead statesman extraordinary honors. Thousands came to gaze upon the countenance of the Great Pacificator as his body lay in state at Washington, Baltimore, Philadelphia, New York, Albany, Buffalo, Cleveland, Cincinnati, and, at length, his well-loved Ashland.

III

JOHN C. CALHOUN

If John C. Calhoun had not quarrelled with Andrew Jackson, when Jackson was president and Calhoun was vice-president, he would have been president of the United States. To become president was the consuming ambition of Calhoun's life. The tragedy of his life was the tragedy of a great mind devoted to a little idea, the right of a state to secede. In his early years in public life Calhoun was a strong Nationalist and Unionist, but in the latter part of his life he devoted himself to an idea which was sectional, rather than national.

Calhoun came of that rugged Scotch-Irish stock which has scored so deep a mark upon the history of the United States. He was born in the Calhoun Settlement near Abbeville, South Carolina, March 18, 1782. After a brief schooling under his brother-in-law, Moses Waddell, in Columbia County, Georgia, he entered the Junior class at Yale College, where he graduated in 1804. He then studied law in the famous law school of Tapping Reeve at Litchfield, Connecticut, was admitted to the bar in 1807, and opened a law office at Abbeville. His marriage in 1811 to Floride Calhoun, daughter of a wealthy second cousin, made him financially independent. His plantation home at Fort Hill, near Abbeville, now stands on the campus of Clemson College.

Calhoun's first speech was delivered at Abbeville in 1805 and was a denunciation of British aggression at the time the British ship *Leopard* fired upon the *Chesapeake* and seized sailors on that vessel. After a short term in the South Carolina legislature, Calhoun was elected to Congress, where he served from 1811 to 1817, when he became Secretary of War in President Monroe's cabinet.

In 1824, at the end of Monroe's second term, Calhoun was one of the chief aspirants for the presidency. The other candidates were Adams, Clay, Crawford of Georgia, and Andrew Jackson. At this time Calhoun was known as a Nationalist, rather than a States Rights man. Adams wrote of him in his diary: "Calhoun is a man of fair and candid mind, of honorable principles, of cool self-possession. He is above all sectional and factious prejudices, more than any other statesman of this Union with whom I have ever acted." But Adams makes the further observation that this was when Calhoun hoped to become president.

In those days no candidate hoped to become president without the endorsement of Pennsylvania, and Calhoun was greatly disappointed when Pennsylvania endorsed Jackson for the presidency and Calhoun for vice-president. In the election of 1824 Calhoun was chosen vice-president by a large majority, nearly all the northern states voting for him. None of the candidates for the presidency had a majority, and John Quincy Adams was elected by the House. Four years later Calhoun allied himself with Andrew Jackson and was again chosen vice-president. It was hard for him to sit as a presiding officer in the Senate as a mere listener to the debates in which he would fain have taken part. His presidential ambitions were well known to everyone. The sharp-tongued John Randolph of Virginia one day commenced one of his vitriolic tirades in the Senate by saying, "Mr.

Speaker! I mean Mr. President of the Senate and would-be president of the United States, which God in His infinite mercy avert!"

Calhoun was the typical Scotch-Irishman—tall, raw-boned, determined-looking. In certain respects there was a resemblance between him and his great adversary, Andrew Jackson. Both men were tall, thin, and angular, and had a mass of thick, gray, bristling hair. Both had remarkable eyes. The thing that observers always noted about Calhoun, and which reveals itself in his portraits, was his piercing, meteor-like eyes. Harriet Martineau, who heard him in the Senate in some of his encounters with Henry Clay, described him as "a somewhat tall, slender-built, ghostly-looking man, about fifty years of age, erect and earnest, with an eye like a hawk's, and hair sticking up like quills upon the fretful porcupine. His voice was harsh, his gestures stiff and like the motions of a pumphandle. Yet there was something in his physiognomy, his brilliant, spectral eyes, his colorless cheek blanched with thought, and his compressed lips that riveted your attention as with hooks of steel." The same Harriet Martineau sketched Calhoun as the "cast-iron man, who looks as if he had never been born, and never could be extinguished."

It was the plan and hope of Calhoun to succeed Jackson after the latter had served one term, but a series of incidents created a complete breach between the two men and crushed Calhoun's hopes of becoming president after Jackson. One of these incidents was the storm which raged in social and official circles at Washington around the attractive Peggy O'Neill, the daughter of the keeper of the inn where Jackson and John Eaton, his Secretary of War, had lived. Peggy O'Neill was first married to a purser in the navy, John Timberlake.

There were rumors that Eaton had been too familiar with pretty Peggy, whose husband died when on duty in the Mediterranean. There was a report that he had committed suicide. Eaton then married Peggy, with the approval and advice of Jackson, who thought this would put an end to the unsavory rumors. But Washington society refused to accept Mrs. Eaton, and referred to her as "Pothouse Peg," and the "Harpy of Degradation." Jackson, who had been stung by the unjust imputations against his own beloved Rachel, took up the cudgels for Mrs. Eaton and tried to force her upon the social and official life of Washington. One of those who refused to receive Mrs. Eaton was Mrs. Calhoun, the wife of Jackson's vice-president. This was with the approval of Calhoun, who afterwards in a public statement spoke of "the great victory that has been achieved in favor of the morals of the country by the high-minded independence and virtue of the ladies of Washington."

Another incident that strained the relationship between Jackson and Calhoun was the disclosure by Crawford, Calhoun's rival for the presidency, that Calhoun, when a member of Monroe's cabinet, had censured Jackson for his conduct in the Seminole War when he seized Spanish military posts. Jackson was enraged at this, and sent a curt note to his vice-president demanding an explanation.

But the real break between the two men was over the nullification theories of Calhoun. In defense of South Carolina, which had protested against the protection tariff bill passed by Congress in 1828, and called the "Bill of Abomination," Calhoun advanced the theory that the Union was a compact of states that might be dissolved by the secession of any one of them, independent of all action on the part of others. He held that the state had power, within its own area, to veto and estop the enforcement of any act by the Federal government which that particular state deemed unconstitutional. Webster held the view that Calhoun did not intend to go the whole length of secession, and did not see that to "begin with nullification, and yet hope to stop short of secession, dismemberment, and revolution was as if one were to take the plunge of Niagara and stop half way down."

Calhoun eventually went back to the old Roman plan of two consuls, one checking the other, and even made the preposterous proposal that the nation have two presidents, one from the slave states and one from the free states, each with the power to veto any act of Congress which was repugnant to one of the two sections.

With the hope of advancing his theories, Calhoun arranged for the famous Jefferson birthday dinner which was held April 13, 1830, at the Indian Queen Inn. Jackson sat at one end of the table and Calhoun at the other. When the time came for the president to speak, Jackson arose, lifted his glass, and looking straight at Calhoun, uttered the celebrated toast: "Our Federal Union! It must and shall be preserved!" After some applause, there was anxious silence, as all waited to see what Calhoun, whose toast came next on the list, would say. Lifting his glass, and his eyes flashing like a meteor, Calhoun said, "Our Federal Union! Next to our liberties, the most dear!"

In 1832 a South Carolina convention adopted an ordinance nullifying the tariff acts of 1828 and 1832. The greatest excitement reigned in South Carolina. Troops were called out and medals were struck bearing the im-

JOHN C. CALHOUN

press, "John C. Calhoun, First President of the Southern Confederacy."

Jackson was never greater than in this crisis. He answered South Carolina's defiance with a courageous proclamation, and made ready to call upon the governors of New York, Pennsylvania, Virginia, North Carolina, Ohio, Tennessee, Alabama, Georgia, and North Carolina for 35,000 men. The vigorous action of Jackson put an end to nullification at that time; but the theories of Calhoun became the doctrine upon which the Southern States seceded in 1860 and in 1861, after the election of Lincoln. There is no doubt that Jackson had under serious consideration the arrest of Calhoun for high treason. He told Robert Letcher of Kentucky, whom the anxious Calhoun had sent to confer with him and learn his intentions, that if another step was taken in the path of nullification he would try Calhoun for treason, and if convicted, "hang him on a gallows as high as Haman."

In the last days of his life, Jackson, dying of consumption, asked his physician,

"What act in my administration, in your opinion, will posterity condemn with the greatest severity?"

The physician answered that perhaps it might be the removal of the deposits from the banks.

"Oh, no!" said Jackson.

"Then it may be the specie circular?"

"Not at all!"

"What is it, then?" asked the physician.

"I can tell you," said Jackson, lifting himself up on the pillows, and his eyes blazing with fire, "I can tell you! Posterity will condemn me more because I was persuaded not to hang John C. Calhoun as a traitor than for any other act in my life."

The break between Jackson and Calhoun destroyed the latter's hope and ambition to succeed Jackson as president. But in the campaign of 1844, he was again an active contestant for the Democratic nomination. In order to avoid any unfavorable reaction to a vote in the Senate on the questions of the day, Calhoun resigned his seat in the Senate, saying it was for the nation to say for how long a time he should be retired from the public service. Newspapers were established in Washington, New York, and South Carolina to promote his campaign.

The nominations were made that year by a national convention at Baltimore, the first held by the Democrats. Calhoun was strongly opposed to the convention method, and at first planned to become a candidate whether nominated by a convention or not. As the weeks passed by, however, it became apparent that he would have no chance at the convention, and he instructed his supporters not to present his name. The leading candidate was Van Buren. But his campaign was shipwrecked by the answer he gave to a question as to the annexation of Texas, which became the burning question with the voters that year. Van Buren avowed himself in favor of the annexation of Texas when it could be brought about with peace and honor, but not at that time, when war with Mexico would ensue. The Southern Democrats who wanted Texas as a new empire for the slave system, to offset the growing power of the Free States, straightway abandoned Van Buren and nominated Polk, who was elected president, defeating the popular Whig idol, Henry Clay, who took an equivocal position on the annexation of Texas.

The campaign of 1844 wrote "finis" to the presidential ambitions of both Henry Clay and John C. Calhoun. The irony of it was that in every respect, by political theory, by devotion to the slave system, by intellectual ability, and by popular esteem in the South, Calhoun was the natural and logical man to ride to the presidency on a campaign for the enlargement of the slave empire. But he had to step aside and see the prize go to the little-known Polk.

Calhoun's last formal speech in the Senate was on March 4, 1850, when the Compromise Measures of Henry Clay with relation to California and New Mexico were under debate. He was so weakened by disease that he was not able to deliver the speech himself, but swathed in flannels, and his eagle eyes half closed, he sat directly in front of Senator Mason of Virginia as he read the speech for him. He was in the Senate again when Webster made his ill-starred Seventh of March Speech, and also when Seward delivered his "Higher Law than the Constitution" speech on March 11.

Calhoun's philosophy of nullification was his obsession to the very end. On the last night of his life, March 30, 1850, he had his faithful clerk read to him from his "Discourse on the Constitution." The next morning he passed away, aged 68. Almost his last words were, "The South! The poor South!" He was buried with a great lamentation in St. Philip's Churchyard, Charleston.

On the 14th of April, 1865, four years to the day after the national flag had been lowered at Fort Sumter, the identical flag was raised again over the smouldering ruins of the Fort by the man who had lowered it and saluted it, General Anderson. A distinguished delegation had gone down to Charleston to take part in the celebration. Henry Ward Beecher made the speech of the occasion. When the party visited St. Philip's Churchyard, where Calhoun is buried, and came to his grave, all the rest stood back and waited to see what William Lloyd Garrison, the great Abolitionist, would have to say at the grave of slavery's greatest defender. Looking down on the grave, Garrison said slowly, "Down into a grave deeper than this slavery has gone, and for it there will be no resurrection."

IV

DANIEL WEBSTER

"The very thought of having Daniel Webster president of the United States should make the heart of any American leap in his bosom and cause him to dream of the days of George Washington."

So wrote Philip Hone, the New York merchant diarist, who knew and entertained most of the notable men of his generation. Today we wonder that the people of the United States passed by such a man as Daniel Webster in electing their presidents.

Born January 19, 1782, in the New Hampshire hills, and a graduate of Phillips Exeter Academy and Dartmouth College, Webster became a national figure when on January 26, 1830, he delivered his famous reply to Robert Y. Hayne, of South Carolina, who had set forth the States Rights and nullification doctrines of John C. Calhoun. This was the speech which concluded with the now memorable sentence, "Liberty and union, now and forever, one and inseparable." Senator Walker of Wisconsin said that when he heard Webster pronounce the word "forever" in that closing sentence, he for the first time in his life became conscious of immortality.

From the year of that great speech until the time of his death, the thought of the presidency was in the mind of the great orator. In 1836 he was nominated by the Whigs of the Massachusetts Legislature as their candidate, but in the election of that year he received only the electoral vote of Massachusetts. He had hoped for the support of the Pennsylvania Whigs in 1840, but anti-Masonry was then a powerful political factor, and as Webster had not come out as strongly anti-Mason as the Pennsylvania Whigs desired, their convention turned to General William Harrison, who had the backing of Henry Clay. Webster gave Harrison his support in the campaign and wrote for him an inaugural address, which Harrison wisely declined to use, saying that the people would know it was Webster's. But he did submit his own address to Webster for criticism and revision. After working all day over the address, Webster came home late for dinner, and his wife, seeing his weary and troubled look, asked him what was the matter—had anything happened? Webster replied, "You would think something had happened, if you knew what I have done. I have killed seventeen proconsuls as dead as marble, every one of them." In the election Van Buren received 170 votes, Harrison 46, and Webster 16.

When Thurlow Weed, visiting Webster at Marshfield in 1848, told Webster that General Taylor would be the next president, Webster exclaimed, "Why Taylor is an illiterate frontier colonel, who hasn't voted for forty years!" Yet Webster had to give way to this illiterate frontier colonel, as he had to yield to Harrison eight years before.

On the seventh of March, 1850, Webster delivered a speech in the Senate in which he condemned the violence of the anti-slavery and abolition forces, admitted that the North had been remiss in returning fugitive slaves, but also said that there could be no peaceful secession. This speech in behalf of the compromise measures of Clay and the Fugitive Slave Act aroused sorrow and indignation among many of Webster's admirers and worshipers in the North, who felt that for the sake of getting the support of the South as a presidential candidate two years hence, he had sold himself and compromised with slavery. Whittier expressed his sorrow and that of many another friend of freedom in "Ichabod— The glory hath departed":

"All else is gone; from those great eyes
The soul has fled;
When faith is lost, when honor dies
The man is dead!

"Then pay the reverence of old days
To his dead fame;
Walk backward with averted gaze
And hide the shame."

The anti-slavery Whigs had been eagerly awaiting the speech of Webster, confident that he would demolish the arguments of the compromisers and all friends of slavery. But to their dismay, instead of arraigning the friends of slavery, he arraigned its opponents and poured his wrath upon the abolitionists of the North. As for the territories under discussion, such as New Mexico and Utah, Webster declared their mountainous and sterile character was a stronger slavery barrier than any possible law passed by Congress. He would not, therefore, attempt to "re-enact the law of God."

Goldwin Smith wrote of Webster at this time: "His character, to which the friends of freedom in the North had long looked up, fell with a crash, like that of a mighty tree, of a lofty pillar, of a rock that for ages had breasted the waves."

In one of his great sermons preached at that stirring period, Henry Ward Beecher, using the same figure of speech that Whittier had employed, the sons of Noah walking backward, exclaimed, "O, Lucifer! Son of the Morning! How art thou fallen! I would not speak harshly of Daniel Webster. . . . The time was when there was no man I so much revered, and for statesman's genius, for stature of understanding, there is no man on the globe, since the death of Robert Peel, who is his equal. No; I would not cast stones at him. I would rather do as did the sons of Noah, and going backward, cast a cloak over his nakedness."

Today the more favorable opinion of Webster is that as a great lover of the Union he felt dismayed at the prospect of its dissolution, and with the difficult choice before him, took the lesser evil of compromise. At a great meeting in November, 1851, in Faneuil Hall, Boston, Rufus Choate advocated Webster, then in Fillmore's cabinet, as the Whig's choice for the presidency. In the convention which met at Baltimore in 1852 Rufus Choate made a brilliant speech in behalf of the compromise policies. When he was charged with trying unfairly to arouse enthusiasm for his candidate, Choate retorted, "Ah, sir, what a reputation that must be, what a patriotism that must be, when you cannot mention a measure of public utility like this, but every eye spontaneously turns to, and every voice spontaneously utters that great name of Daniel Webster."

General Winfield S. Scott and President Fillmore led in the ballots, but Webster was always a powerful candidate, and Whig leaders had agreed that if Webster could get as many as 41 pledged votes from the North, the Fillmore men would go over to him. But William H. Seward, strong anti-slavery Whig, who controlled the New York delegation, could not be moved. Scott was nominated on the fifty-third ballot, and in the ensu-

DANIEL WEBSTER

ing election was humiliatingly defeated by Franklin B. Pierce, who had been an inconspicuous junior officer under Scott in his Mexican campaign. When the telegraphic message from the convention was put in Webster's hands, and he opened it and read, "Scott 159, Fillmore 112, Webster 21," his only remark was, "How will this look in history!" Today it does indeed look strange that the author of the Reply to Hayne and of the Bunker Hill Oration should have been passed over by the convention for men like Scott and Fillmore.

Enemies of Webster who held that in his Seventh of March Speech, 1850, he had sold himself to the South, gloated over the fact that in the Whig convention he did not receive a single southern vote. This they said was his due reward.

Soon after the Baltimore convention, a crowd gathered in front of Webster's Louisiana Street home at Washington. They had come to celebrate the nomination of Scott, but also to cheer Webster. Webster went out on the balcony of his house and said to the serenaders: "Gentlemen, I will tell you one thing. You may be assured that there is not one among you who will sleep better tonight than I shall. I shall rise tomorrow morning with the lark, and though he is a better songster than I am, yet I shall greet the purple east as jocund, as gratified, and as satisfied as he."

But that was for public consumption. In reality Webster was deeply chagrined and disappointed. Rufus Choate hurried from Baltimore to Washington and found him disconsolate and too despondent to speak about the nomination. Choate said that the supper he had with him was like a first meal after the family returns from the cemetery when the shock of the bereavement is recognized for the first time. On a train a few days later, a friend asked Webster whether, after all, the presidency could have been of any value to him. Webster replied that perhaps he was just as well without that office. "But, sir," he added, "it is a great office. Why, Mr. Bates, it is the greatest office in the world, and I am but a man, sir. I want it! I want it!"

Webster had supported both Harrison and Taylor, but Scott was too much for him. When a friend wrote him just a few days before his death, expressing the hope that he would not change his mind about not supporting Scott in the campaign, Webster said, "Write to him and tell him to look over towards Charlestown and see if the Bunker Hill monument is still standing."

Even if he had been nominated, Webster could not have been elected, for he died at Marshfield, October 24, 1852. As he lay on his death bed during those last days, he had a ship's lantern hung at the top of the mast of a little yacht on which he kept the stars and stripes flying, so that even in the night he could see that the flag, upon which his eloquence had cast such lustre, was still there.

V

WILLIAM H. SEWARD

The most amazing upset in the history of American politics was the defeat of William H. Seward at the Republican Convention in 1860, when Lincoln was nominated. The fact that was uppermost in the minds of the delegates as they returned from Chicago, and in the mind of the country at large, was not that Lincoln had been nominated, but that Seward had been defeated. In the speech which he made at the convention, seconding the motion to make the nomination of Lincoln unanimous, Carl Schurz said that the name of William H. Seward would "remain in history an instance of the highest merit uncrowned with the highest honor."

How did it come about that the man nearly everyone in the Republican party regarded as representing the highest merit was "uncrowned with the highest honor"? What was the explanation of the overthrow of Seward at the Chicago Convention, a man who was the embodiment of the intellectual power, the moral zeal and courage, the eloquence and determination of the new party of freedom? "It was from Governor Seward," said William Evarts at the Chicago Convention, "that most of us learned to love Republican principles and the Republican party."

Born May 16, 1801, at Florida, New York, amid the beautiful hills of Orange County, Seward graduated at Union College in 1820. He read law in an office at Goshen, New York, and in 1822, with $50.00 in his pocket from his father, set out for Auburn, then the chief town in New York west of Albany. There he married his law partner's daughter, and threw himself with industry and enthusiasm into the business, social, political, and religious life of the community. In 1830, during the anti-Mason agitation, Seward was elected to the State Senate on the anti-Mason ticket. In 1838 he was elected Whig governor of New York, re-elected in 1840, and served as governor until 1843. During his term as governor, Seward recommended a measure providing for the establishment of schools where the children of foreigners could be instructed by teachers speaking the same language as themselves and professing the same faith. This proposal aroused the opposition of the anti-Catholics, and twenty years afterwards rose up like a ghost to stand between Seward and the nomination for the presidency.

In 1849 Seward was elected to the United States Senate. The next year he attracted the attention of all parties in the country by his "Higher Law than the Constitution" speech. The speech followed that of Webster's famous "Seventh of March" speech on the compromise measures, particularly with regard to the admission of California with a free constitution, and territorial governments for other lands taken from Mexico, without any provision as to slavery. Seward did not mean that the higher law was contrary to the Constitution, but that the Constitution and the Divine Law were in agreement; but the phrase "higher law" appealed to the popular imagination, and henceforth Seward became known as the man who held that the Constitution was binding only when it was in accord with the laws of God. This "Higher Law" speech made him the particular object of Democratic and Southern

WILLIAM H. SEWARD

hatred. Lincoln at that time, far behind Seward in his stand on the slavery question and moving with the greatest caution, said that "Seward's speech, insofar as it may attempt to foment a disobedience to the Constitution, has my unqualified condemnation."

In 1855 Seward formally allied himself with the newborn Republican party, and henceforth was everywhere recognized as the real Republican leader. In the campaign of 1858, speaking at Rochester, New York, Seward delivered his famous "irrepressible conflict" speech, in which he said of the agitation over slavery: "It is an irrepressible conflict between opposing and enduring forces, and it means that the United States must and will, sooner or later, become either entirely a slave-holding nation or entirely a free labor nation." It was four months afterwards that Lincoln expressed the same idea in his "House divided against itself" speech before the Republican State Convention at Springfield.

At the first Republican Convention at Philadelphia, in 1856, Seward was passed over for the fantastic Pathfinder, Fremont.

Had he been nominated, as he deserved to have been, at that Republican Convention, he undoubtedly would have been the candidate in 1860 and would have been president.

Seward felt that his political partner, Thurlow Weed, had deserted him at that convention for Fremont. One day, long after the War, when Seward and Weed were riding together up Broadway and were passing Lincoln's statue at Union Square, Seward, pointing to the statue, said, "Weed, if you had been faithful to me, I should have been there instead of Lincoln." "Seward," answered Weed, "is it not better to be alive and in a carriage with me, than to be dead and set up in bronze?"

When the Chicago Convention convened, there seemed to be little doubt as to the nomination of Seward. On the first ballot Seward had 173½ votes, Lincoln 102. On the third ballot Seward had 180 votes, Lincoln 231½. Of the votes that Lincoln had picked up after the first ballot, the largest block came from Pennsylvania, which gave him 52 votes on the third ballot. The Pennsylvania leaders at the convention declared that the nomination of Seward would cost the Republicans Pennsylvania and Indiana. It was feared that those who had adhered to the American, or Know-Nothing, party in Pennsylvania and Indiana would not support Seward because of the attitude he had taken twenty years before when governor of New York on the school question and the Catholic question. There is little doubt today that these leaders were mistaken, and that Seward would have carried Pennsylvania and Indiana by as large majorities as Lincoln did.

Another factor in the defeat of Seward was the enmity of his old friend and colleague, Horace Greeley, who managed to get to the convention as a delegate from Oregon. Greeley, Seward, and Thurlow Weed had long been associated in New York State politics. Greeley could never forget that after the campaign in 1837, when he edited a paper for Seward and Weed, he was passed over and neglected by his political partners when the spoils of offices were distributed. At the Chicago Convention he used his great influence, not to nominate Lincoln, for Bates was the candidate he preferred, but to defeat Seward. When the result of the third ballot was announced, showing Lincoln leading Seward by 51 votes, a smile of satisfaction played across the rustic, moonlike face of the great editor. Remember that smile, and you have one of the chief reasons for the defeat of Seward.

Another factor in the overthrow of Seward, according to James G. Blaine, was the place where the convention was held. "Had the convention been held in Albany," said Blaine, "Seward would have been nominated."

Seated on the spacious lawn of his Auburn mansion, Seward waited for the news of his nomination. The townsfolk had brought a cannon to his gate, loaded and primed, ready to be fired the moment the wires brought the tidings of his nomination. Soon after the third ballot had been taken at Chicago, a telegram giving the result was handed to Seward. His fine, sharp-cut face paled. Lincoln had been nominated! The crowd of friends dispersed, and the cannon was hauled off unfired.

The Republican party and the nation held its breath after the convention to see how Seward would take his defeat. But one of the finest chapters in his life was the way in which he accepted his overthrow by the country lawyer of Illinois. He took the stump in behalf of Lincoln, became his chief adviser in the critical period between the election and the inauguration, and as Secretary of State rendered a service to the Republic and to human liberty which can never be forgotten. When Lincoln was assassinated by Booth, Seward, too, was marked for death and was cruelly stabbed at the same hour by one of the conspirators, Lewis Payne. Three days later, Seward, swathed in bandages, and propped up with pillows, saw from his window the great black catafalque with its nodding, sable plumes, as the funeral cortege of Lincoln passed down the street.

Only once did Seward give expression to the keen disappointment and chagrin he felt over his defeat at the Chicago Convention. Potter of Wisconsin, who was pressing Carl Shurz for the appointment as Minister to Spain, said to Seward that if Schurz were not appointed it would be "a great disappointment" to many people in the country. Leaping to his feet, and pacing the floor excitedly, Seward exclaimed, "Disappointment! You speak to me of disappointment! To me, who was justly entitled to the Republican nomination for the presidency, and who had to stand aside and see it given to a little Illinois lawyer! You speak to me of disappointment!"

VI

SALMON P. CHASE

"Of all the great men I have ever known, Chase is equal to about one and a half of the best of them."

That was Lincoln's estimate of his great Secretary of the Treasury, and the man who thought he could make a better president than Lincoln. Salmon P. Chase was born January 13, 1808, in a yellow house at Cornish, New Hampshire. It was sometimes said by people in that neighborhood that the Yellow House was more famous than the White House, and that more brains had been born in it than in any other house in New England. After graduating from Dartmouth College, to which he had been admitted by answering the question, "Where do the Hottentots live?" Chase read law in the office of eloquent William Wirt, and in 1829 commenced the practice of his profession at Cincinnati.

Intensely religious, studious and industrious, Chase soon made a name for himself as an able lawyer and as a friend of fugitive slaves. He defended John VanZandt, the original of John Van Tromp, of "Uncle Tom's Cabin," on the charge of harboring and concealing a fugitive slave. In this case, which was tried before the United States Supreme Court, Chase made the friendship of Governor Seward of New York. In a short time he and Seward were everywhere regarded as the brains and organizers of the political anti-slavery movement. When a mob came raging up to the doors of the Franklin House at Cincinnati to lynch James G.

44

SALMON P. CHASE

Birney, editor of an anti-slavery paper, it was Chase who stood in the doorway and cowed the mob with his courage.

In 1852 a coalition of Free-Soilers and Democrats sent Chase to the United States Senate from Ohio. There he took part in the great debates over the Kansas-Nebraska Bill, which, in effect, repealed the Missouri Compromise of 1820, prohibiting slavery north of 36 degrees, 30 minutes, in the territory of the Louisiana Purchase. When Chase heard the roar of the cannon fired to celebrate the passage of the bill, he said to Charles Sumner, with prophetic foresight, "They celebrate a present victory; but the echoes they awake will never rest till slavery itself shall die."

In 1855 Chase was elected the first Republican governor of Ohio. The Republican party in 1856 was not quite ready for a man of Chase's outspoken opinions with regard to slavery, and chose for its standard bearer the fantastic and romantic Fremont. But when the Republican Convention of 1860 met at Chicago, Chase and Seward were the most spoken of in connection with the nomination. To Carl Schurz, who stopped at Columbus shortly before the Chicago Convention, Chase frankly avowed his ardent desire to be president. Schurz warned him that if the Republican Convention had courage enough to nominate an anti-slavery man, "they will nominate Seward. If not, they will not nominate you." Chase received only 49 votes in the balloting and felt keenly that the Ohio delegation had not supported him with unanimity. Writing to a friend after the convention Chase said, "I am quite content that it fell to Mr. Lincoln, not that I believe he will prove more available than I should have been, or that his nomination is a wiser one than that which you favored—pardon this egotism."

Lincoln at once made Seward Secretary of State and Chase Secretary of the Treasury. The extraordinary thing is that Chase, who had almost no financial experience, and had devoted much of his time and energies to the writing of anti-slavery declarations, and the organization of anti-slavery parties, became our greatest Secretary of the Treasury since the days of Alexander Hamilton. A defeat on the battlefield was not necessarily fatal to the Union, but a defeat in the Treasury Department would have meant national ruin. Somewhat against his own financial principles, Chase yielded to the necessity of the occasion, and on February 25, 1862, resorted to the Legal Tender Act, authorizing the issue of 150,000,000 of United States notes called "greenbacks" because of the green ink used in printing them.

Lincoln was but a child in financial matters, so much so, that once at the White House, producing a five dollar greenback note, and pointing to the inimitable signature of the registrar of the Treasury, L. E. Spinner, he said to Ward Lamon, "No one will ever be able to counterfeit it." To Lamon's astonishment, the president evidently thought that Spinner wrote his name on every bill! Lincoln's chief contribution to the solution of the country's financial difficulties was a jest. When a plan to put on the greenbacks some kind of a motto, similar to the "In God We Trust" on the silver coins, was being discussed, Lincoln, asked his opinion, said, "If you are going to put a motto on the greenbacks, I would suggest that of Peter and John, 'Silver and gold have I none, but such as I have give I thee.' "

It is to Chase that we owe the familiar "In God We Trust" on the national coins. Chase wrote to James Pollock, then director of the mint at Philadelphia, and a godly Presbyterian elder, that "the trust of our people in God should be declared on our coins. You will cause a device to be prepared, without unnecessary delay, with a motto expressing in the fewest and tersest words possible this national recognition."

Chase was the great advocate of a Proclamation of Emancipation, and rejoiced in his soul when Lincoln finally decided to issue the Proclamation after the victory at Antietam. It was Chase who wrote the closing sentence of the Proclamation, in which Lincoln is made to say, "And upon this Act I invoke the considerate judgment of mankind and the gracious favor of Almighty God."

Chase earnestly desired the presidency and was sincerely convinced his election would serve the country better than the re-election of Lincoln. We see Lincoln today through the halo of martyrdom, for the flash of the assassin's pistol lifted him to the rank of a demigod. Any contemporary who entertained an opinion other than the highest concerning the man of sorrows who sits enthroned in the beautiful white temple on the banks of the Potomac at Washington is likely to be discounted by the people today. It is difficult for us now to understand or appreciate the intense opposition that there was among able and patriotic Americans to the re-election of Lincoln.

Horace Greeley, the *Tribune's* "thunderer," felt that the country would be ruined if Lincoln continued his policies, and referring to the part he had played in the nomination of Lincoln, and how it was frequently said that but for Greeley's campaign against Seward, Lincoln would not have been nominated, said, "It was a mistake. The biggest mistake of my life." There were many other strong patriots who thought Lincoln as president was a great mistake. Some were impatient with Lincoln's conservative methods of dealing with the slavery question; others were angry that he gave important military commands to men like McClellan who were not strong in their anti-slavery feeling. Others were impatient with Lincoln's jokes, and felt that a man who could read Artimus Ward to his cabinet when a great decision was to be made was unfitted for his high post.

It was only natural that opponents of Lincoln should have thought of Chase, who had won the battle for the Union in finances. Chase was a man of magnificent physique and appearance, and his head and face, which men liked to compare with that of Daniel Webster, stamped on the greenbacks, made him one of the best known men of his day. More than anyone then in public life, he looked the great man. To a friend Chase wrote that he felt that with God's blessing he could administer the government of this country so as to secure and "imper-dibilize" our institutions. To General Ben Butler, whom he sounded out as to running on his ticket as vice-president, Chase described himself as a man witnessing a destructive fire and unable to do anything to extinguish it.

Yet in seeking after the presidency, Chase scorned to make any improper use of the vast patronage at his disposal as the Secretary of the Treasury. When told that a certain appointment would help his presidential chances, Chase wrote, "I should despise myself if I were capable of appointing or removing a man for the sake of the presidency."

To friends who protested to Lincoln against Chase seeking the presidency while he was in the cabinet, Lincoln replied with one of his humorous stories. A lazy horse with which he and his brother were once plowing a field suddenly rushed across the field with such speed that Lincoln with his long legs could hardly keep up with him. On reaching the end of the furrow, he found an enormous chin fly fastened on the horse and knocked him off. But his brother protested, saying, "Why, that's all that made him go!" "Now," said Lincoln, "if Mr. Chase has a presidential chin fly biting him, I am not going to knock him off, if it will only make his department go." To another who complained of Chase's presidential activities, Lincoln replied, "If he becomes president, all right. I hope we may never have a worse man."

But to more intimate friends Lincoln betrayed the fact that he was quite anxious about Chase's activities. Colonel Alexander McClure says that Lincoln's anxiety for a renomination was the thing ever uppermost in his mind during the third year of his administration, and that he never saw Lincoln unbalanced except during the fall of 1863 when Chase was making his honest and sincere efforts to win the nomination. The matter came to a head when one of Chase's backers, Senator Pomeroy of Kansas, issued, without Chase's knowledge, a circular in which it was stated that Lincoln's re-election was impossible, even if desirable; that his tendency toward compromise would be stronger in a second term than it had been in the first; and that in Chase were united more of the qualities needed in a president during the next four years than were combined in any other candidate. When this circular got into the newspapers, Chase wrote to Lincoln expressing his readiness to withdraw from the Treasury. Lincoln at that time declined to accept his resignation.

The Chase boom came to an end in February, 1864, when the Union members of the Ohio Legislature held a caucus and nominated Lincoln for re-election. But in the summer of 1864, when the chances of Lincoln's re-election seemed meagre, prominent Republicans, such as Whitelaw Reid and Charles Sumner, launched a movement to have Lincoln withdraw. Then another convention was to be called and Chase nominated. But the military victories of Sherman and Sheridan changed the whole political situation and no further efforts were made to have Lincoln withdraw.

Chase withdrew from the Treasury in June, 1864, having taken offense because Lincoln refused to name for the post of Assistant Treasurer of New York a man whom Chase had recommended. The resignation of Chase caused consternation in the Senate, and a committee of Senators at once waited on Lincoln, asking that the resignation be reconsidered. Lincoln, evidently glad to have Chase out, said, "I will not longer continue the association. I am ready and willing to resign the office of president and let you have Mr. Hamlin as president, but I will not longer endure the state I have been in." At the same time, however, Lincoln expressed the view that when he had opportunity he would make Chase Chief Justice of the United States. This opportunity came in October, 1864, when the aged Chief Justice Taney, notorious because of his Dred Scott decision, died.

Chase soon discovered that he was unhappy and dissatisfied as Chief Justice, and his presidential aspirations began to revive. In this he was ably seconded by his beautiful daughter, Kate Chase Sprague, whose tragic divorce from her wealthy husband, Senator William Sprague, who in a jealous mood attacked with a pistol his children's German tutor and Senator Roscoe Conklin, was a national sensation in the 'seventies and the early 'eighties. Kate Chase was one of the few women in the history of the United States who exerted real political influence, and all who knew her paid tribute to her beauty and extraordinary charm.

Chase hoped that in 1868 he might receive the Republican nomination, and was especially anxious that Ohio should endorse him. But Grant was nominated and the name of Chase was not presented. Chase's friends then turned to the Democrats, and an active campaign, led by his beautiful daughter, was waged in his behalf at the New York Convention. But again he was disappointed, for the Democrats named Governor Horatio Seymour.

Even after 1870, when Chase had been stricken with paralysis, his daughter Kate arranged for receptions at his home, "when he was gotten up," says Carl Schurz, "to show that he was still physically fit, and made futile and pathetic attempts to appear youthful and vigorous." The end came on May 7, 1873, when death, which stills all fevers, wrote "finis" to the presidential, and all other earthly ambitions of Salmon P. Chase.

VII

STEPHEN A. DOUGLAS

Douglas, the Little Giant, was one of the great Americans who did not reach the White House; but in a dramatic gesture of loyalty to the Union he held the hat of his successful rival, Abraham Lincoln, when he delivered his inaugural address.

Like Clay, Webster, Blaine, and Bryan, Douglas had an immense popular following in the nation, and at one period was undoubtedly the best known American. Yet, as in the case of the men just named, his popularity could not avail to make him president.

The political doctrines of Stephen A. Douglas were anathema to the people of New England, yet he was reared in the Green Mountains, having been born at Brandon, Vermont, April 23, 1813. His physician father died when Douglas was an infant. As a youth he drifted about from one home to another, from one school to another, and from one apprenticeship to another, finally going West, and in 1833, not yet twenty-one years of age, opened a law office at Jacksonville, Illinois, just fifty years before another famous aspirant for the presidency, William Jennings Bryan, opened a law office in the same town.

The young lawyer at once took an interest in politics, became State Attorney, Judge of the Supreme Court, member of the Legislature, and in 1847 United States Senator from Illinois. In the same year he married Martha Denny Martin, a daughter of Colonel Robert

Martin, a well-to-do planter and slaveholder of Rock-
ingham County, North Carolina. Douglas' foes often
charged that his attitude toward the slavery question
was influenced by his personal interests in the "peculiar
institution." Douglas, however, had refused the gift
of a plantation from his father-in-law, saying that he
did not wish to be responsible for the slaves. The year
of his marriage Douglas moved to Chicago, where he
made heavy and profitable investments in Chicago real
estate.

As a member of the Senate in 1850, Douglas supported the compromise measures of Henry Clay and
also the Fugitive Slave Act. By 1852, although only
thirty-nine years of age, he was one of the candidates
for the Democratic nomination for the presidency. The
other candidates were General Lewis Cass, James Buchanan, and Franklin Pierce. To the astonishment of
the country, Pierce, a respectable and honorable nobody,
the intimate friend of Nathaniel Hawthorne, was nominated and elected president. On one ballot, the thirty-
first, Douglas had the highest vote of all the candidates.

The popular sobriquet by which Douglas was known,
the "Little Giant," was bestowed upon him after one
of his first political speeches, and it implied the combination of littleness of stature, for he was but five feet one
inch tall, and bigness of intellect. Harriet Beecher
Stowe, who heard him speak in the Senate, described
him as the "very ideal of vitality, short, broad, and
thick-set. He has a good head and face, thick black
hair, heavy black brows and a keen eye." John Quincy
Adams was much disgusted when he first heard Douglas
speak in Congress, and in his diary records how he raved
and roared and worked himself into a frenzy of excitement and gesticulation. "In the midst of his roaring,

STEPHEN A. DOUGLAS

to save himself from choking, he stripped off and cast away his cravat, unbuttoned his waistcoat, and had the air and aspect of a half-naked pugilist."

By 1854 the agitation over the slavery question had subsided, and the country was in the midst of prosperity. It was then that Douglas brought forward the bill which split his own party, destroyed the Whig party, and hastened the outbreak of the Civil War. This was the Kansas-Nebraska Bill, which provided for the division of the vast western territories into Kansas and Nebraska, with the provision that all questions relating to slavery should be left to the decision of the inhabitants of these territories. This was, in effect, the repeal of the Missouri Compromise of 1820, which, outside of Missouri, prohibited slavery north of latitude 36 degrees 30 minutes in the territories of the Louisiana Purchase.

No measure was ever introduced into Congress which produced such a stir in the nation. The Abolutionists and the Anti-slavery Democrats of the North, and all others opposed to slavery rallied to denounce the bill. Public meetings were held all over the North and the bill was arraigned as "a gross violation of a sacred pledge, as a criminal betrayal of precious rights." But Douglas fought the bill through the Senate and the House and it became law in March, 1854. Douglas now found himself the object of execration and denunciation. He said he could have traveled from Boston to Chicago by the light of his own burning effigies. He was saluted as Judas Iscariot and Benedict Arnold. A group of pious women in an Ohio village sent him thirty pieces of silver as a token of their esteem. On the night of September 1, 1854, Douglas attempted to address his constituents in front of the North Market Hall in Chicago. When he rose to speak he was greeted with hisses and jeering which drowned his voice. After fronting the mob for two hours, he took his watch from his pocket, and seeing how late the hour was, cried out in a moment of quiet, "It is now Sunday morning—I'll go to church, and you may go to Hell!"

Douglas survived the abuse and unpopularity which followed his advocacy of the Kansas-Nebraska Bill, and in 1856 was again a candidate for the Democratic nomination. He was defeated by the courtly James Buchanan, whose chief "availability" lay in the fact that he had not been in the country during the fierce debates over the Kansas-Nebraska Bill. Douglas had 122 votes in the convention to 168 for Buchanan. In that same year Douglas married the lovely Adele Cutts, a reigning belle of Washington and a grand-niece of Dolly Madison. His first wife had died in 1852, and her passing had an unfortunate effect upon Douglas, who became careless in his habits and shabby in his dress. After the death of his first wife, Douglas had taken a long trip abroad, not only to the countries usually visited by American travelers, but to Russia and the Near East.

Douglas broke with the administration and with his party when he denounced the Lecompton Constitution which had been proposed for the people of Kansas, a constitution which practically would have compelled the people to accept slavery. The next year, 1858, he was renominated for the Senate by the Illinois Democrats. Lincoln was the Republican candidate, and the celebrated Lincoln-Douglas Debates ensued. There is little doubt that the stature which Lincoln has achieved in our national history has colored the story of those debates, and somewhat discounted the ability and success of Douglas. In the give and take of a popular debate, Lincoln was no match for Douglas; but when it came to principles and moral issues he had the advantage. In answer to the question of Lincoln, Douglas said, and seemed not at all reluctant to say, that while he upheld the Dred Scott decision which recognized slavery in the territories, the ultimate decision was with the people of the territories, whether they wanted slavery or not. This was his doctrine of "popular sovereignty." It did not satisfy the anti-slavery people of the North, neither did it satisfy the old-time Democrats of the South. Lincoln had the majority of the popular vote, but the districts were so arranged in the state that Douglas carried the election in the state Senate.

Douglas had said that he didn't care whether slavery was voted up or down in the territories so long as popular sovereignty was recognized, and Lincoln rejoined, "But I care, and God cares." It is altogether probable that had Douglas "cared" more on the subject of slavery, and had taken a more consistent position, not only advocating popular sovereignty but attacking the Dred Scott decision, he could have been the nominee of the Anti-Slavery Democrats and the Republicans as well; and if so, he would have been president of the United States. Indeed, there were prominent Republican leaders who had conferences with him at that time.

The Democratic National Convention met at Charleston in April, 1860. When the convention adopted as part of its platform the principle of non-interference on the part of Congress with regard to slavery in the territories, the old-line Democrats bolted the convention. After fifty-seven futile ballots the convention adjourned to Baltimore, where, on June 23, Douglas was nominated. The old-line Democrats who had bolted the convention nominated John C. Breckenridge, and the Constitutional Union nominated John Bell of Tennessee.

Thus the Democratic party was rent in twain and the election of Lincoln was practically assured.

Douglas created quite a sensation as a presidential candidate by going on the stump himself, speaking in New England, the Northern states, and in the South. When at Cedar Rapids he learned that in the October elections Pennsylvania had gone Republican, he said to his secretary, "Mr. Lincoln is the next president. We must try to save the Union. I will go South." In spite of threats of personal violence, he invaded the South and did what he could to persuade the Southern Democrats to accept the inevitable. When asked if it would be in order for the Southern States to secede in case Lincoln was elected, he gave an emphatic and courageous "No," and an equally courageous and emphatic "Yes," when asked if the Government had the right to oppose by force such a secession. In the election Douglas got the electoral vote of just one state, Missouri, and three of the seven votes of New Jersey. But his popular vote, and he was the only candidate to get votes from all sections of the country, was just 489,495 less than that of Lincoln.

During the campaign, Seward, who was on the stump for Lincoln, and whose remarkable speeches played an important part in the success of the Republican candidate, was in his sleeping car when the train stopped at Toledo. Charles Francis Adams, son of the minister to England, who was traveling with Seward, heard someone rush into the car and inquire in a loud voice, "Where's Seward?" The speaker was Douglas. When Seward's berth had been pointed out, Douglas thrust the curtains aside and exclaimed, "Come, Governor, they want to see you. Come out and speak to the boys." Seward answered from the depths of his bed, "How

are you, Judge? No, I can't go out; I'm sleepy."
"Well, what of that," said Douglas, "they get me out
when I'm sleepy." When Seward still refused to get
up, Douglas answered, "Well, if you don't want to,
you shan't." As he left the car he drew a bottle of
whiskey and added another drink to those which he
evidently had already taken. General McClellan, who
at the time of the Lincoln-Douglas Debates was vice-
president of the Illinois Central Railroad and traveled
with Douglas on a special car, tells how before the address at Bloomington he found Douglas unkempt and
sleepy after all night amusements with his friends, and
had him retire to his private cabin so that he could pre-
pare himself for his speech.

After the election of Lincoln, Douglas did all that he
could to prevent the secession of the Southern States
and the outbreak of the War. On the day of Lincoln's
inauguration he let it be known that he would make
himself conspicuous during the ceremonies, so that the
people of the country would know how he stood. He
was sitting on the platform near Lincoln when the
president-elect arose to deliver his speech. Lincoln was
looking about for a place to deposit his high hat, when
Douglas with a smile reached out his hand and, taking
the hat, held it for him during the delivery of the
inaugural address.

After the fall of Sumter, Douglas made a much pub-
licized call on Lincoln and urged him to call out 200,000
troops instead of 50,000. He was frequently after this
in consultation with Lincoln, and at Lincoln's request
traveled through the country delivering speeches in behalf of the Government and the Union. The most memorable of these was on April 25, in the capitol at
Springfield. Men who heard that speech remembered

it to their dying day. In Chicago he was conducted to the Wigwam where Lincoln had been nominated, and there delivered another great speech in behalf of the Union. In that speech he said, "There are only two sides to the question. Every man must be for the United States or against it. There can be no neutrals in this war—only patriots, or traitors."

Soon after this speech he was stricken with typhoid fever. In his delirium he cried out, "Telegraph to the president and let the column move on!" On June 5, 1865, murmuring to his wife to tell his sons to support the Constitution of the United States, the Little Giant, one of the greatest of the great Americans who attained not unto the presidency, passed into the land where all contention, and all ambition, is stilled.

VIII

GENERAL GEORGE B. McCLELLAN

General George B. McClellan might have been president of the United States had he come openly out for Lincoln and his administration during the critical period of the Gettysburg campaign in 1863. That was the verdict of America's most astute politician, and its greatest president-maker, Thurlow Weed, who said to a friend in 1880, when the name of McClellan was mentioned, "He might have been president as well as not."

General George B. McClellan was born in Philadelphia, December 3, 1826, the third child of a distinguished Philadelphia physician, Dr. George McClellan. He graduated at West Point in 1846 and served with great distinction in the Mexican War. After the war he was an instructor in military engineering at West Point, and translated French military works into English. In 1851 he accompanied his future father-in-law, and his Chief of Staff in the Civil War, Captain R. B. Marcy, in an expedition up the Red River to Arkansas. This was followed by an expedition to survey a route for a railroad across the Cascade Mountain. Jefferson Davis, the Secretary of War, appointed McClellan to go abroad and study the operations of the armies in the Crimean War. One of the results of McClellan's trip abroad was the introduction of the McClellan Saddle, still used in our army. In 1857 McClellan left the army and became vice-president of the Illinois Central Railroad, in which capacity he frequently met Abraham Lincoln, a counsel for the road.

When the Civil War broke out, McClellan was president of the Ohio and Mississippi Railroad, with headquarters at Cincinnati, at a salary of $10,000 a year. Pennsylvania and Ohio both sought his services in the organization of their troops. McClellan accepted the Ohio offer and a month later was made a Major-General in the United States Army and placed in command of the Department of the Ohio. In the campaign of Rich Mountain, western Virginia, he defeated the Confederate Army under Garnet with a victory which electrified the whole country. Henceforth he was known as the "Little Napoleon." After the defeat of Bull Run, July 21, 1861, he was summoned to take command of the troops in and about Washington. There he organized a great army, which became known as the "Army of the Potomac." The finest tribute that can be paid to the creative and organizing ability of McClellan is the history of the Army of the Potomac, how it survived disaster after disaster in the field, unbroken in spirit and undiminished in its power to strike. Many waters of adversity and floods of defeat could not quench its magnificent spirit.

McClellan's first great campaign was the Peninsula Campaign, when he took the Army of the Potomac by water to Yorktown and marched up the Peninsula towards Richmond. There is every reason to believe that McClellan would have been successful in that campaign, and that the rebellion would have been put down two years before it was, if he had not been hampered and hindered by Lincoln and badgered and betrayed by Stanton. The military records available today leave no doubt as to the disloyalty of the Secretary of War, Stanton. The largest division in the Army of the Potomac, McDowell's, at the last moment was detached from McClellan's Army.

The then Confederate Commander, Joseph E. Johnston, was quick to take advantage of this opportunity and to attack McClellan's divided army at Fair Oaks. When Lee succeeded Johnston, and in command of a Confederate army that was larger than at any time during the history of the war, he attacked McClellan in a series of bloody battles, known as the Seven Days' Battles, as McClellan withdrew down the Peninsula and changed his base from the York River to the James. But McClellan had inflicted heavier losses upon Lee than he himself had suffered, and his army, still in splendid spirits and well organized, was only a short distance from Richmond. But the anxious Lincoln, guided now by the impossible and stupid Halleck, took McClellan's army away from him and put it under the command of General Pope. Pope's army was almost destroyed in the second battle of Bull Run. When that disorganized and broken army was tumbling in on Washington, and everything seemed lost, Lincoln, with Halleck, came early on the morning of September 2 to McClellan's home in Washington, and asked him to take charge of the troops around Washington and "save the country."

McClellan's magic name and beloved personality and his genius for organization soon restored the Army of the Potomac to a high pitch of efficiency. He followed Lee in his invasion of Maryland, and on the seventeenth of September, 1862, the bloodiest single day of the war, so damaged Lee's army that the Confederate commander withdrew across the Potomac. This great victory was followed by the preliminary Proclamation of Emancipation. Because of the political and interna-

GENERAL GEORGE B. McCLELLAN

tional influence of that Proclamation, Antietam was, in a sense, the decisive battle of the Civil War.

Sitting one day after the battle on a hillside at Antietam, and with his long legs propped up and his knees under his chin, Lincoln said to McClellan, "General, you have saved the country twice. You must remain in command and carry us through to the end." But within a month, on November 7, 1862, just as he was about to engage Lee's army again in Virginia, and with every prospect of victory, he was relieved of his command and ordered to proceed to Trenton, New Jersey, "to await orders" which never came.

At the end of that year, 1862, Lincoln had an interview with Thurlow Weed, the powerful New York politician, and revealed the greatest depression as to the military and political situation, especially the political, as Seymour, the powerful anti-administration Democrat, had carried New York in the November elections. At the request of Lincoln, Weed went to see Governor Seymour, and gave him the message that if he would stand by the Administration and place himself at the head of a great Union party, Lincoln would stand aside at the next presidential election and help put him in the White House. Seymour seemed to assent; but when he issued his message to the New York Legislature, instead of praising Lincoln and calling for soldiers, he denounced the Administration.

Having failed in his overtures to Seymour, Lincoln then turned to McClellan, still a Major General, and still waiting orders at Trenton. "Tell the General," Lincoln said to Weed, "that we have no wish to injure or humiliate him; that we wish only for the success of our armies. That if he will come forward and put himself at the head of a Union Democratic party, and through that means push forward the Union cause, I will gladly step aside and do all I can to secure his election in 1864."

Weed also suggested to McClellan that he preside at a great Union Democratic Mass Meeting to be held in Union Square on June 16, 1863, when Lee's army was moving into Pennsylvania. McClellan, unfortunately for his political future, declined to preside at the meeting, although telling Weed that the war must be prosecuted to save the Union and the Government, at whatever cost of time, treasure, and blood.

McClellan let his great opportunity slip. Weed was America's most astute politician and president-maker, and there is no reason to doubt the correctness of his opinion when he said, "If McClellan had presided at that war meeting, and had persistently followed it up, nothing but death could have kept him from being elected president of the United States in 1864."

In 1864 McClellan was nominated for the presidency by the Democratic Convention in Chicago. Unfortunately, the Convention was under the domination of bitter anti-administration men like the notorious, but brilliant, "Copperhead," Clement L. Valandingham. It was Valandingham who drafted the platform with its fatal plank that the "war was a failure." McClellan accepted the nomination, but repudiated the platform, saying that he could not look into the face of his comrades of the army and navy who had survived so many bloody battles and tell them that their labors and sacrifices had been in vain.

In spite of the disloyal platform of the Democratic party, it looked for a time as if McClellan would be elected. There had been great dissatisfaction with Lincoln among Republican leaders. General James A. Garfield, who had just entered Congress, wrote, "We hope we may not be compelled to push Lincoln for four years more," and Whitelaw Reid, in the *Cincinnati Gazette*, described Lincoln as ready to surrender the cause of human freedom to the masters of slave plantations. Grant and General Rosecrans were both suggested as men to succeed Lincoln. Chase, too, the powerful Secretary of the Treasury, was an open candidate for the nomination.

As the summer wore on after Lincoln's nomination, the Republican leaders began to get anxious. Lee had stopped Grant in one of the bloodiest repulses of the war at Second Cold Harbor, June 3, and the people were growing weary of the slaughter and the long deferred victory. So anxious were the Republican leaders, that Francis P. Blair, Sr., even before McClellan's nomination, went to him and besought him to refuse to let his name be presented at the Democratic Convention, and to ask Lincoln for another command in the army. He plainly intimated to him that if he did so, he would have immense prestige in the country and his political future would be the brightest. But McClellan had reason to think that he could be elected in the campaign of 1864 without waiting for another four years.

By the end of August Lincoln himself was so pessimistic as to his chances in the approaching election, that after getting a discouraging report from the chairman of the Republican National Executive Committee, Henry J. Raymond, Editor of the *New York Times,* he submitted one day to his Cabinet a folded paper and asked them to write their names across the back of it, giving no intimation of what he had asked them to endorse. After his reelection he took the paper from his desk one day at a meeting of the Cabinet and let them know what he had written and what they had endorsed. It was this:

"This morning, as for some days past, it seems exceedingly probable that this administration will not be reelected. Then it will be my duty to so co-operate with the president-elect as to save the Union between the election and the inauguration, as he will have secured his election on such grounds that he cannot possibly save it afterwards."

The victories of Sherman at Atlanta, of Farragut at Mobile Bay, and of Sheridan in the Shenandoah Valley, knocked the planks one by one out of the Democratic platform, dissipated the gloom of Lincoln, and made certain his reelection. McClellan carried just three states, New Jersey, Delaware, and Kentucky. The soldiers in the army cheered for McClellan, but most of them voted for Lincoln. Yet a shift of 250,000 votes would have given McClellan the popular majority, and a change of 50,000 votes in some of the doubtful states would have meant his election.

Nothing can change the verdict of Lincoln after Antietam that McClellan had "saved the country." But had McClellan listened to the advice of Thurlow Weed, or to the advice of Francis Blair, Sr., and given his support to Lincoln and his administration, there is no doubt that he could have been president. He, therefore, is perhaps the only man in the history of the nation who both sought after the presidency, and yet refused it when it knocked at his door.

IX

HORACE GREELEY

The saddest tragedy in the history of the great men who sought the presidency and missed it was the campaign of Horace Greeley. His defeat killed him. Few of our presidents have occupied such a prominent place in the public eye or so influenced their day and generation as did Horace Greeley, the editor of the *New York Tribune.* Greeley is one of the most marked personalities of our history. He was born at Amherst, New York, February 3, 1811, the son of a poor, hardworking farmer. He was apprenticed as a youth to the editor of a paper at East Poultney, Vermont. As a lad he walked nearly the whole distance across the state of New York to Clymer, in Erie County, where his father had settled. He tried his hand as a printer at Jamestown and Gowanda, and in the summer of 1831, when he was twenty years of age, arrived in New York and got a job in a printing house setting up a commentary on the Book of Genesis and one on the New Testament. He was discharged from his first newspaper job with *The Evening Post,* because the editor wanted only "decent looking men in the office." Even at that early age, Greeley was somewhat grotesque in his appearance.

After a series of magazine and newspaper adventures, most of them unfortunate, Greeley, in 1838, was chosen by William H. Seward and Thurlow Weed, New York's president maker, to edit the *Jeffersonian,* a campaign journal. In the campaign of 1840, when Harrison defeated Van Buren, Greeley edited for the Whigs a campaign weekly called *The Log Cabin,* which had extraordinary success. It was in this campaign that the signing of patriotic songs at political meetings had its origin. Greeley ran these songs in his *Log Cabin.*

In 1841 he established the *New York Tribune,* destined to become the most powerful journal in America. In thousands upon thousands of homes the *Tribune,* especially the *Weekly Tribune,* was the political Bible. Through its columns Greeley profoundly influenced the thinking of America in one of the most critical periods of its history. The *Tribune* barred police reports, scandals, and medical and theatrical advertisements, but introduced book reviews and lectures. Associated with him in one capacity or another was Albert Brisbane, the disciple of Charles Fourier, and the father of Arthur Brisbane, the famous columnist of recent times; Charles A. Dana; Bayard Taylor and Margaret Fuller.

Greeley early espoused the Free Soil and Anti-slavery movement. He was an important figure in the first important Republican Convention held at Pittsburgh on Washington's Birthday, 1856. The Kansas excitement was then at its height. In his paper Greeley had advocated resistance to the Fugitive Slave Act and had assisted in arming the Kansas Free Soilers. But in his speech at the Pittsburgh Convention, in contrast with such men as Joshua R. Giddings, he was singularly restrained.

Greeley was a great traveller. On a visit to Paris in 1855 he spent two days in jail on a debt charge. This experience he rated as one of the most instructive of his life: "There are many ways of studying human nature; many diverse lights wherein this motley world is or may be contemplated; I judge that one of the most

HORACE GREELEY

instructive glimpses of it is that which we obtain through grated windows. . . . I am quite sure that one of the most wholesome and profitable, though least pleasant, experiences of my life, is that afforded by my confinement for forty-eight hours (with a good prospect of permanence) in the spacious debtors' prison in Paris."

In the years 1852-1853, some public-spirited citizens planned a World's Fair in New York and constructed an enormous edifice at Sixth Avenue and 42nd Street. The site of the Exposition was too far uptown for that day, and it was a failure from the beginning. Greeley was a director and, in a small way, a bondholder. P. T. Barnum was the chief figure in the enterprise. When Greeley arrived in Paris in 1855, he was put under arrest at the suit of a Parisian sculptor, who alleged he had contributed to the New York Exposition a statue which had been broken, and for which he claimed of Greeley as a director $2500. The court refused the security offered by Don Piatt, Secretary of the American Legation, and Greeley was haled to prison. Judge John Y. Mason, our ambassador then at Paris, called upon Greeley in the prison, and after talking with him said, "I have heard you called a philosopher, and I now see that you deserve the distinction." After a tedious legal squabble Greeley was released. In 1859 he made his famous trip to California, returning by way of Panama. The impressions of this journey are found in his "*An Overland Journey from New York to San Francisco in the Summer of 1859.*"

In the Republican Convention at Chicago in 1860, Greeley, sitting as a delegate from Oregon, played an important part in the defeat of William H. Seward and the nomination of Abraham Lincoln. For over twenty years Greeley had nursed a grievance against Seward because Seward and Weed, after using Greeley's editorial ability in political campaigns in New York, had passed him by when the spoils of office were distributed. By this time Greeley, with his half moon face fringed with whiskers, his shapeless clothes and shambling gait, his high pitched, squeaky voice, and his illegible scrawl, was a national character, looked upon with a "mixture of admiration and affectionate amusement." Parton thus describes Greeley's appearance: "In walking he swings or sways from side to side. Seen from behind he looks, as he walks with head depressed, bended back and swaying gait, like an old man. But the expression of his face is singularly and engagingly youthful. His complexion is extremely fair and a smile plays ever upon his countenance. . . . I have seen Horace Greeley on Broadway on Sunday morning with a hole in his elbow and straws clinging to his hat. I have seen him asleep while Alboni was singing her grandest. He is a man that could save a nation, but never learn to tie a cravat, no, not if Brummell gave him a thousand lessons."

When the Civil War broke out he ran at the mast head of the *Tribune* the famous slogan, "On to Richmond!", and thus helped to create the national sentiment which pushed the Northern Army into the disastrous campaign of Bull Run. Greeley always defended himself against the charge that this slogan was the impulse to disaster, and held that the Confederate Congress should never have been permitted to meet in Richmond on the 4th of July, 1861.

His somewhat unstable nature was manifested in a letter he wrote to Lincoln after the disaster at Bull Run. In this letter he said: "You are not considered a great man, and I am a hopelessly broken one. . . . Can the rebels be beaten after all that has occurred? If they can—and it is your business to ascertain and decide—write me that such is your judgment, so that I may know and do my duty. And if they cannot be beaten, if our recent disaster is fatal, do not fear to sacrifice yourself to your country. If the rebels are not to be beaten, then every drop of blood henceforth shed in this quarrel will be wantonly, wickedly shed, and the guilt will rest heavily on the soul of every promoter of the crime.

Yours in the depths of bitterness, Horace Greeley."

Like many others, Greeley was impatient with Lincoln for his slowness in moving towards emancipation. When after the victory at Antietam Lincoln finally issued the Proclamation, Greeley hailed it as "recreating the nation."

In 1864 Lincoln sent Greeley on a futile peace embassy to Niagara Falls. He was against the renomination of Lincoln because he felt that the country needed a man of greater drive and energy. After the Civil War Greeley made himself somewhat notorious in the North by signing in 1867 the bond of Jefferson Davis. This cost him thousands of subscribers to the *Tribune*. He opposed the reelection of Grant, partly because of his advocacy of one term for the president, and partly because of his dissatisfaction with the policies of Grant and the political machine headed by Conkling which backed Grant.

In 1872 the Liberal Republican Convention, meeting at Cincinnati, nominated him for the presidency over Charles Francis Adams, who had been the favorite candidate of reformers like Carl Schurz. In July the Democratic Convention, meeting in Philadelphia, also nominated Greeley as its candidate. The campaign was one of great bitterness. Greeley was denounced as a traitor to his party and pilloried as a fool and an ignoramus. Although everyone else saw that he was doomed to defeat, Greeley up to the last was confident of his election. One of his chief friends and supporters, Colonel A. K. McClure, said he was entirely confident of success, and that he had never seen a happier face than that of Greeley's. But John Bigelow significantly said: "Greeley, I think, is destined to learn the difference between notoriety and popularity. Greeley is an interesting curiosity which everyone likes to see and to show, and in whom we all feel a certain kind of natural pride; but I do not think anyone can seriously believe in his fitness for any administrative position whatever."

Senator George F. Hoar described the nomination of Greeley by the reformers as "ludicrous and preposterous." Almost every attack he made on the first administration of Grant was answered by the regular Republican stump speakers with a quotation from Greeley in the *New York Tribune*. The southern people never felt unkindly towards Grant and resented more what Greeley had said as a politician than what Grant had done as a soldier. The speeches which Greeley delivered were recognized as some of the ablest political utterances that the country had ever heard, but he had no chance against the hero of Appomatox and its famous apple tree. He was overwhelmingly defeated in the election and did not carry a single northern or western state. So bitter and vituperative was the campaign, that Greeley once remarked that he did not know whether he was running for the presidencey or the penitentiary.

To the tragedy of his rejection by the American people was added the tragedy of his practical dismissal from the editorship of the *New York Tribune,* for when he went back to his office after the campaign he found that Whitelaw Reid had become the real editor of the paper.

But saddest of all was the death of his wife, who died October 30. For days and nights Greeley had tenderly nursed her. Six days later came the overwhelming defeat at the polls. Crushed by his multiplied sorrows, Greeley's great mind broke down and he died insane at a sanatorium on November 29, 1872. Immediately, the nation which had ridiculed him and lampooned him, and yet respected him and loved him, turned to do him honor. Grant, the president, and Wilson, the vice-president, attended his funeral, and thus gave public expression to the nation's sorrow over the man whom it had covered with odium and ridicule.

X

SAMUEL J. TILDEN

If in 1877 David Davis, who had been Lincoln's close friend and backer, and now a member of the Supreme Court, had not been elected by the Democrats and Independents of Illinois to the Senate, Tilden would have been president of the United States.

The Democrats in Congress had supported the Electoral Commission Bill at the time of the dispute over the election of Hayes and Tilden with the expectation that Davis would serve as the fifth Justice on the Commission. It was known that he was favorable to Tilden, and his vote on the Electoral Commission would have given the election to Tilden, just as the vote of Justice J. T. Bradley, who was named in Davis' place, gave the election to Hayes.

Samuel J. Tilden was sixty-two years of age when he was nominated by the Democrats for the presidency. He had made a good record as a reform governor in New York, and had gained national reputation through his overthrow of the corrupt Tweed political ring in New York. He was an exceedingly successful corporation lawyer, and it was said that at one time half the great railroads of the country were his clients. He had amassed a fortune, and was the wealthiest man ever to run for the presidency.

But in many respects Tilden was a most unlikely presidential candidate. He had a strong analytical mind, but not a powerful or attractive personality. His appearance was not impressive, his voice was feeble, and his movements nervous and awkward. In the crisis which followed the election he showed himself lacking in leadership and in resolution. His association with large corporations, his great wealth, and his alleged use of money for political purposes, could hardly have been regarded as an asset for a presidential nominee, and certainly there was nothing in his voice or his "pinched, bloodless features" that would arouse the enthusiasm of voters. William M. Evarts, Tilden's classmate at Yale, said that if elected he would be the phantom of Buchanan's likeness in the presidential chair.

A contemporary thus describes Tilden: "A man of modest, unobtrusive personality, stooped, and hence looked smaller than he is—small, smooth boyish face—round head, bent with that sleepy droop in the left eyelid . . . caused by ptosis . . . small, delicate, utterly unobtrusive features . . . dressed with a plainness . . . like the pettiest clerk . . . so weak, so mild, so selfless, so uncombative . . . surrounded by political giants, who bow before the modest, little man with the cold, passionless, sagacious face."

Born at New Lebanon, New York, where his father was postmaster and storekeeper, and a local politician of some influence, Tilden spent one brief term at Yale College, attended for a time New York University, and also the Law School of the University; was admitted to the bar in 1841 and opened a law office at Number 11 Pine Street. He soon attained prominence at the bar, and also as a writer of political pamphlets. When the Civil War broke out, Stanton, who succeeded Cameron as Secretary of War, called Tilden to Washington and sought his advice, which was to call out the full military

SAMUEL J. TILDEN

strength of the North at once and crush the rebellion by one powerful blow, what today would be called in German warfare a "blitzkrieg."

After the war, Tilden, as chairman of the New York State Democratic Committee, exposed and prosecuted the William M. Tweed Ring, which had controlled city politics in New York. In 1874 he was elected governor of New York, in which office he broke up another corrupt political combination known as the Canal Ring, a crowd of politicians of both parties who were enriching themselves by the money spent in extending the state canal system.

In 1876 Tilden's New York reforms had so fired the imagination of the country that he was nominated at the Democratic Convention for the presidency. The great advantage that he had in the campaign was the odor of graft and corruption that hovered about Grant's second administration. Tilden himself was in poor health, and some of his backers thought that he showed a singular lack of interest in the election. He was dubbed 'Slippery Sam," and "Tilden and his Barrel" appeared in many cartoons. These cartoons showed Tilden pouring a barrel of money into a ballot box.

Tilden was attacked during the campaign respecting his income tax return. A rich man, he returned only $7,118 as his income for 1862 and 1863. It was charged that in 1862 he had a net income of $89,000 and had cheated the Government out of more than $4,000. Tilden met the charge by saying that his income producing property was largely in railroad stocks and bonds and other securities on which the tax was deducted by the companies before the interest and dividends were paid. Nast, the great cartoonist of the day, depicted Tilden timid and shrinking between two fires. On one side a

Union soldier, and on the other a Confederate, demands, "Whose side were you on?" The answer given was, "I . . . I . . . was busy in court with a railroad case." This cartoon reflected on Tilden's absence from the ranks during the Civil War, and the charge that he made himself rich as a "railroad wrecker." There was much waving of the "bloody shirt," charges of outrages on the negroes, and a new Solid South conspiracy. Senator Wheeler declared on the stump, "Let your ballots protect the work so effectually done by your bayonets at Gettysburg."

Tilden made only two non-political addresses during the campaign, one at the Centennial at Philadelphia, where he was given a big ovation.

On Wednesday morning, November 8, nearly all the newspapers in the country, with the exception of the *New York Times* and the *New York Herald,* which said that the result was in doubt, announced the election of Tilden. James A. Garfield explained the Democratic victory as a result of the "combined power of Rebellion, Catholicism, and Whiskey." This was the forerunner of Dr. Burchard's "Rum, Romanism, and Rebellion."

The *New York Times* gave Tilden 184 votes and Hayes 181, but said Florida was doubtful, and if Hayes received the four votes of Florida, he would have a majority of one. At half past ten P.M. on Wednesday, November 8, the Republican National Committee at the Fifth Avenue Hotel issued a bulletin saying that Louisiana, Florida, South Carolina, Wisconsin, Oregon, Nevada, and California had given Republican majorities, and that this insured the election of Hayes. There was the greatest public excitement, and for several days crowds of men, neglecting their business, hung about the bulletin boards of the newspapers.

The managing editor of the *Times,* John C. Reid, after a conference with Zach Chandler and W. E. Chandler at the Fifth Avenue Hotel, hurried to the office of the Western Union, and, under the name of Zach Chandler, the National Chairman, sent telegrams to trustworthy Republicans in South Carolina, Florida, Louisiana, Oregon, and California. The telegram read, with variations: "Hayes is elected, if we have carried South Carolina, Florida, and Louisiana. Can you hold your state? Answer immediately." This was in the early morning of November 8, the day after the election. Hayes wrote in his Diary the night of the election, "From that time I never supposed there was a chance for Republican success."

The dispute settled down to Oregon, Louisiana, South Carolina, and Florida. There was no claim or pretense in any quarter that the Republicans did not have a lawful majority of the votes cast for electors in Oregon, but the Democrats claimed that one of the electors was a postmaster, and that he had not resigned his office, as he ought to have done, before he was chosen an elector.

As the excitement increased over the dispute about the returns sent in from Louisiana, South Carolina, and Florida, there were threats of Civil War. Henry Watterson in the *Louisville Courier* declared that 100,000 armed citizens would march on Washington to maintain the rights of Tilden. A Republican member came to Henry B. Paine, Representative from Ohio, and with tears in his eyes said, "We shall be cutting one another's throats in this chamber before the 4th of March." When in the House a Democrat from Virginia declared that they had come to the place where one side or the

other must make "an ignominious surrender or we must
fight," and asked, "Are the gentlemen prepared for the
latter alternative?" a loud roar of "Yes" went up from
the Republican side of the House.

Montgomery Blair became editor of *The Daily Union,* established in Washington, December 6, 1876, to
lead the movement for Tilden's inauguration. "Tilden
or blood" was a slogan among reckless Democrats.
Tilden and Hendrix minute-men were enrolled and military organizations formed in eleven states. Generals
Corse, Franklin, and Hancock were mentioned as possible commanders-in-chief.

It was the retrospective judgment of Senator George
F. Hoar, who served on the Electoral Commission, that
"but for the bitter experience of a few years before,
with its terrible lesson, there would have been a resort
to arms. It would have been a worse Civil War than
that of the Rebellion, because the country would have
been divided, not by sections, but by parties." President
Grant took strong measures in the crisis and ordered the
military to protect the Election Board canvassers, saying, "No man worthy of the office of president should
be willing to hold it if counted in or placed there by
fraud."

In the latter part of January, 1877, wise and mod-
erate men, disturbed over the situation, finally devised
a plan for the appointment of an Electoral Commission.
The Electoral Commission was composed of three Republicans and two Democrats from the Senate, three
Democrats and two Republicans from the House, also
five of the Justices of the Supreme Court, four of them,
two Republicans and two Democrats, designated in the
Bill, and these four Justices were to choose a fifth, who
would thus have the deciding vote between the seven

designated Republicans and the seven designated Democrats. Justice David Davis was to have been named the fifth Justice on the Commission, and it was with the expectation of his appointment that the Democrats had supported the Bill in Congress. But in the meantime Davis was elected to the Senate by Illinois, and Justice Joseph T. Bradley took his place. In every dispute the Commission voted for the Republican electors by a strictly party vote, 8 to 7.

On the second of March Hayes was declared elected president. He took office on Saturday, March 3, because the fourth fell on a Sunday, and Grant's term would have expired before the public exercises on March 5. There was some anxiety lest Hayes should be assassinated. One of the most dependable historians of that period, Colonel A. K. McClure, said, "There were grave fears that Hayes would be assassinated at the inauguration, more so than there were for Lincoln. Every precaution was taken to protect Hayes on his journey from Ohio to Washington."

Hayes had taken a high position during the critical months of this disputed election. Writing to John Sherman of Ohio soon after the election, Hayes said: "A fair election would have given us 40 electoral votes in the South, at least that many. But we must not allow our friends to defeat one outrage by another. There must be nothing curved on our part. Let Mr. Tilden have the place by violence, intimidation, and fraud, rather than undertake to prevent it by means that would not bear the severest scrutiny."

Tilden showed himself a poor leader during the crisis. He was probably still suffering from the effects of a cerebral attack in 1875. Tilden's infirmity of purpose was a great handicap to his party. If he had issued an address to the some four millions who had voted for him, announcing that he would maintain his rights, and that if the Republicans did not yield there would be civil war, he might have entered the White House. Blaine afterwards said that if the Democrats had been firm the Republicans would have backed down.

In the opinion of Abram S. Hewitt, chairman of the Democratic National Committee, Tilden "threw the presidency away," because he would not sign a letter Hewitt had written, addressed to the American people, in which Tilden was to say that he believed himself to be the president-elect, and that on the Fourth of March, 1877, he would come to Washington to be inaugurated.

As late as May 13, 1878, after Hayes had been in office more than a year, a Democratic member from New York introduced a Resolution for the appointment of a committee to investigate alleged frauds in the states of Louisiana and Florida in the recent presidential election. This Resolution was adopted by the House, and it was expected that the committee would make a report denying the validity of Hayes' title, and that the House would be advised to refuse to acknowledge him as president. The Republican leaders in the Senate were preparing to fight this dangerous action of the House, when the Democratic leaders gave up the battle. A determining factor with them, no doubt, was the discovery that an attempt had been made by followers of Tilden to bribe members of the Canvassing Boards of the disputed states. Dispatches indicating such attempts at bribery had been sent in cipher to Colonel W. T. Pelton, Tilden's nephew, who lived with him at 15 Gramarcy Park, New York. Tilden himself disclaimed any personal knowledge of these messages.

Tilden died in 1886, leaving his fortune, amounting to some six million dollars, for the establishment of a library for the City of New York. When certain Tilden heirs contested the will, the New York Court of Appeals invalidated the clause establishing the Tilden Trust, the object of which was the creation of a free library. But afterwards another settlement was made and the great library of New York City stands today as a monument to the generosity and foresight of the man whom millions of American citizens thought had been robbed of the presidency.

XI

JAMES G. BLAINE

After coming out from a reception at the White House, in 1878, James G. Blaine exclaimed to his sister-in-law, Gail Hamilton: "My God! What is there in this place that anyone should want to get into it!" Yet, none tried harder than Blaine to get into the White House.

A sneer at a fellow member in the House of Representatives on an April day in 1866 cost James G. Blaine the presidency.

"Blaine! Blaine! James G. Blaine!" For twenty years that was the most popular political cry of America, and yet the man who inspired it, and who had a popular following in the country equalled only by that of Henry Clay and William Jennings Bryan, missed the presidency. The influence of Blaine helped to make Hayes president, and made Harrison president in 1888; but he himself was never able to grasp the great prize.

Although Blaine and Maine were almost synonymous, Blaine was not a New Englander by birth. He was born at West Brownsville, on the Monongahela River, in Washington County, Pennsylvania, January 31, 1830. At the age of thirteen he entered Washington College, now Washington and Jefferson, where the students called him "nosey" Blaine because of the prominence of that part of his physiognomy. After a brief experience as a teacher in Kentucky and at the Pensylvania Institute for the Blind in Philadelphia, Blaine entered the field of journalism at Augusta, and afterwards at Portland, Maine. Henceforth it was "Blaine of Maine."

Blaine's political ambitions had first been stirred when as a young teacher in Kentucky he heard Henry Clay speak at Lexington in 1847. At the first Republican Convention in Philadelphia in 1856, Blaine acted as a secretary. In 1863 he was elected to the House of Representatives, where he served for thirteen years. When the mighty Thaddeus Stevens died, a member of Congress asked Blaine one day who could take Stevens' place. Blaine answered that there were three young men of great ability coming to the front in the Republican party. Asked who these three might be, Blaine pointed first to Allison of Iowa, then to Garfield of Ohio, and then, looking up at the ceiling, remarked, "I don't see the third." But the country was soon to see him.

In a discussion in the House over some military bill, Roscoe Conkling, the brilliant and conceited Representative from New York, offended Blaine. Blaine retorted with the sneer that cost him the presidency. Speaking of Conkling he said: "His haughty disdain, his grandiloquent swell, his majestic, supereminent, overpowering, turkey-gobbler strut, has been so crushing to myself and all the members of this House, that I know it was an act of the greatest temerity for me to venture upon a controversy with him." Henceforth, Conkling was the man with the "turkey-gobbler strut," and the newspapers always cartooned him in that posture. As politics go, this sneer was a piece of supreme

JAMES G. BLAINE

folly on the part of Blaine, as he was one day to discover.

When the Convention of 1876 drew nigh, Blaine was the most available and popular of the Republican leaders. He had, however, one serious handicap. The Democrats in the House, aided and abetted by Blaine's foes within his own party, made the charge that in 1869, when Speaker of the House, Blaine had made a decision which saved a land grant for the Little Rock and Fort Smith Railroad, and afterwards had sought favor from the railroad and had disposed of the railroad's bonds at a secret and very liberal commission. The facts as to this transaction were supposed to be contained in the letters which were in the possession of a man named Mulligan. Blaine refused to deliver the letters over to the House committee appointed to investigate the matter. But in a dramatic scene, just nine days before the Republican Convention met in Cincinnati, he read the Mulligan letters himself in the House and produced a powerful impression of his innocence. Yet with his enemies this disposal of the case by Blaine raised unfortunate questions, for, they said, if the letters contained nothing that was incriminating, why should Blaine have hesitated to hand them over to the committee?

The Sunday before the Convention met in Cincinnati, Blaine swooned on the steps of his church. This, too, was an unfortunate incident in connection with his candidacy. Other candidates before the Convention were Rutherford B. Hayes of Ohio, Roscoe Conkling of New York, Bristow of Tennessee, and Governor Hartrantf of Pennsylvania. There was another unfortunate incident, too, in connection with Benjamin F. Bristow, a candidate with a considerable following. When Bristow called at Blaine's home to express his sympathy when he learned of his illness, some unwise member of Blaine's household, looking upon Bristow as a rival candidate, told him that neither Blaine nor the family was at home. Bristow felt this keenly, and at the Convention turned his delegates to the support of Hayes. George F. Hoar, Senator from Massachusetts, says in his autobiography, "If Bristow had not visited Blaine's house that Sunday morning, Blaine would, in my opinion, have been the nominee for the presidency."

Blaine was nominated in a famous speech by Robert G. Ingersoll, then not so notorious, as later, for his hostility to revealed religion. It was this speech that gave Blaine his sobriquet, "The Plumed Knight." "Like an armed warrior," said Ingersoll, "like a plumed knight, James G. Blaine marched down the halls of the American Congress and threw his shining lance full and fair against the brazen forehead of every traitor to his country and every maligner of his fair reputation."

On the first ballot Blaine had 285 votes, and his nearest rival, Morton of New York, 124. On the seventh ballot Rutherford B. Hayes, who on the first ballot had just 61 votes, was nominated.

When 1880 came round, Blaine, now in the Senate, and still tilting with Roscoe Conkling, was once again the leading candidate for the nomination. Grant, just welcomed home with great ovations after his tour of the world, yielded to the persuasion of his friends and permitted his name to go before the Convention for a third nomination and a third term. Roscoe Conkling placed Grant in nomination with a speech that swept the Convention. There had been some critical questions as to what state Grant represented—Missouri, Illinois, Ohio, where he was born, or New York, where he lived. Standing on a press table, Conkling commenced thus:

"And asked what state he hails from,
Our sole reply shall be—
He comes from Appomattox
And its famous apple tree."

On the first ballot Grant had 304 votes. Blaine was second with 284. Grant's faithful 304 clung to him through thirty-six ballots. On the thirty-sixth ballot, James A. Garfield, who on the thirty-third ballot had just one vote, received 399 votes and the nomination. Nearly all his votes had been taken from the Blaine column.

The always generous Blaine entered Garfield's Cabinet as Secretary of State, and was with Garfield when he was shot passing through the Pennsylvania Station at Washington on July 2, 1881.

Before Garfield appointed Blaine his Secretary of State, he asked him point blank if he intended to be a candidate for the presidency in 1884, intimating that he would not put him in the Cabinet if such were his intentions. Blaine answered, "No."

In 1884 it looked as if the twice foiled Blaine and his opportunity had met at last. He was nominated on the fourth ballot at the Convention, which met in Chicago, June 3, 1884. John A. Logan of Illinois, perhaps the most successful of the non-professional soldiers on the Northern side in the Civil War, was nominated as his running mate. The Democrats nominated Grover Cleveland, who had made a good record as a civil service reformer as Governor of New York.

The campaign which followed was one of extraordinary bitterness. A group of distinguished Republicans called Mugwumps, led by Carl Schurz, bolted the ticket and supported Cleveland. Blaine was assailed as a corruptionist and the old Mulligan Letters scandal was revived. Cleveland's moral character was assailed. When charged with misconduct he instructed his managers to tell all and hide nothing. Henry Ward Beecher took the stump in behalf of Cleveland, partly because he did not trust Blaine, and partly because he himself had passed through great agony through charges against his moral character in the celebrated Tildon trial. In his speech at the Cleveland meeting, Beecher said, "I vowed that if God would bring the day star of Hope, I would never suffer brother, friend, or neighbor to go unfriended, should a like serpent seek to crush him." At the same meeting Beecher read a letter which Cleveland had written to Mrs. Beecher, who had inquired of him as to the truth of the reports concerning his character. This frank letter produced an immense impression.

At the time of the Maria Halpin scandal about Cleveland, a man in Kentucky notified Daniel Lamont, Cleveland's private secretary, that he had knowledge of incidents in the private life of Blaine which would be injurious to him as a candidate for the presidency. At Cleveland's direction Lamont sent for the man. When he had submitted his documents, Cleveland asked him if all his proofs had been presented. When the man said that nothing had been kept back and that most of the documents were certified copies of public records, Cleveland sent for Lamont and directed him to pay the man's expenses and send him home. He then took the papers that the man had submitted and the letter that he had sent to Lamont, and tore them into small bits. When he had done this, he sent for his porter and told him to burn the scraps of paper in the fireplace. When the flames had consumed the scandalous documents, Cleveland said to Lamont, "The other side can have a monopoly of all the dirt of the campaign."

Although the battle was close, it was generally expected that Blaine would be elected. If he had gone directly to his home in Maine after his successful tour on the stump, he might have been president of the United States.

Blaine's Roman Catholic associations, and the revival of charges against his personal character, had suggested to some of his backers a reception by Protestant ministers. B. F. Jones, the Pittsburgh steel king, was Chairman of the Republican National Committee, but Senator Elkins, of West Virginia, was Blaine's campaign manager. Elkins advised against the reception and urged Blaine to continue on his way to Maine. Had he taken Elkins' advice, the issue might have been different.

The original plan was to have Dr. Tiffany, an able and prominent divine, make the address to Blaine. Tiffany had been a candidate for the United States Senate in 1855, and had been a leader of the American, or Know-Nothing, Party, when he was connected with Dickinson College. But there was considerable opposition to Dr. Tiffany among the ministers, and it was finally arranged that the oldest minister present should make the address. Dr. S. T. Burchard, a Presbyterian, happened to be the oldest minister and had been speaking only a few minutes, when he discharged his famous, three-barreled alliteration, that in fighting the Democratic Party "Blaine was fighting the party of "Rum, Romanism, and Rebellion." [1]

Blaine's mother was a Catholic, although his father was a Presbyterian, and he himself was a member of the Congregational Church. On his way to New York after campaigning in the West, he had stopped to visit his sister, a mother superior in a convent in Indiana. But all these Catholic facts about Blaine's family were submerged in the flood which broke loose over Dr. Burchard's alliteration. Blaine at first paid little attention to the matter. It was only when he learned that Catholic Churches were to be flooded with circulars on the following Sunday, that he tried to undo the damage. It was thought by many that this unfortunate sentence by the Presbyterian preacher lost Blaine many Catholic votes in New York, which, by the closest of votes, went to Cleveland.

But probably the enmity of Roscoe Conkling, who had never forgotten Blaine's "turkey-gobbler" sneer of twenty years before, was a more determining factor than Burchard's alliteration. For the first time in years Conkling's own county, Oneida, went Democratic.

Blaine lost New York by 1,049 votes. A change of 525 votes would have given him New York and the election. Cleveland carried the country by 62,683 votes. The three closest presidential elections, since the election of Polk in 1844, who won by a plurality of 38,184, were those of 1876, when Hayes defeated Tilden, 1884, when Cleveland defeated Blaine, and 1916, when Woodrow Wilson defeated Hughes.

---

[1] James A. Garfield's statement in 1876 when he thought that Tilden had defeated Hayes, that the Democratic victory was the result of the "combined power of rebellion, Catholicism, and whiskey" may have given Dr. Burchard the cue for his alliteration.

A banner displayed at a Democratic celebration in Morristown, New Jersey, had the following comment on the causes of Blaine's defeat:

"The *World* says the Independents did it,
The *Tribune* says the Stalwarts did it,
The *Sun* says Burchard did it,
Blaine says St. John did it,
Roosevelt says the soft-soap did it,
We say Blaine's character did it.
But we don't care who did it—
It's done."

Blaine, always calm, unshaken, and magnanimous, accepted his defeat as an appointment of Divine Providence, and dismissed all other explanations of his defeat with the comment, "I am fated not to be president."

XII

ROBERT M. LA FOLLETTE

Had Robert M. La Follette come on the scene as a presidential candidate twenty years later than he did, it is quite probable that he would have been elected president of the United States. As an independent candidate in 1924, he received a larger vote than any independent candidate in the history of presidential elections. In 1912 Theodore Roosevelt, the Pregressive Republican candidate, received a vote of 4,125,000; but in 1924 La Follette, 4,800,000. This was an extraordinary tribute to La Follette, for the almost five million people who voted for him did so despite the knowledge that they could not elect him.

La Follette was born June 14, 1855, in a log cabin in Dane County, Wisconsin. He came of French Huguenot stock. At the University of Wisconsin he came under the influence of that notable teacher and philosopher, John Bascom. Soon after graduation La Follette was admitted to the bar and began to practice law in Madison. During his college years he was noted as an orator, winning the inter-state oratorical contest with a striking oration on Shakespeare's "Iago." His wife, Belle Case, was a classmate at the university and ardently supported him and forwarded him in his political ambitions.

In 1880 he was elected district attorney of Dane County, and in 1884 was elected to Congress, serving in the House of Representatives from 1885 to 1891, when a political landslide swept him out of office. One reason for the landslide in Wisconsin was the feeling against the Bennett Law, which had been enacted by the last legislature, and which required that all schools should give a part of their instruction in the English language. This roused the enmity of Lutheran and Roman Catholic suporters and caused an overwhelming Democratic victory in Wisconsin. George W. Peck, humorist, and celebrated as the author of "Peck's Bad Boy," was elected governor. Peck's humorous stories, and his familiar figure, with eye glasses, red carnation, gray moustache and goatee, made him a popular candidate.

The Republican party in Wisconsin at that time was controlled by the very able John C. Spooner and Philetus Sawyer, an Oskosh lumberman and United States Senator. Sawyer offered La Follette employment in defending a suit brought by the Democratic state government against former state treasurers, for whom Sawyer had been the bondsman. When the case came to trial in the court of Judge Robert Siebecker, La Follette's brother-in-law, La Follette created a great sensation by announcing that Senator Sawyer had tried to bribe Judge Siebecker through him, offering him large fees for a favorable decision. Sawyer claimed ignorance of the relationship of La Follette to Judge Siebecker, who withdrew from the case. La Follette was convinced that the whole political situation in Wisconsin was corrupt, and that this corruption was vested chiefly in the caucus and convention system. In 1896, and again in 1898, he was defeated in the Convention for the nomination for governor and charged that corrupt use of money had accomplished his defeat.

During these years La Follette had made himself a familiar figure to the people of Wisconsin. At barbecues, at county fairs, and Chautauqua gatherings, he would be seen standing in the tailend of a wagon, coat off and collarless, fists clenched, denouncing the Wisconsin bosses and the railroads. Although short of stature, La Follette was a most impressive figure on the stump, living up to his sobriquet, "Fighting Bob." He was a consummate actor. Indeed, the stage had been his first ambition in university days, but when he went to consult a well known tragedian, he discouraged him because of his short stature. His histrionic abilities served him well on the platform and on the stump, but he was always in dead earnest. Those who heard him speak can never forget it, and will always remember him with his flashing dark eyes, the high pompadour hair, and the broad and lofty forehead.

So successful had his campaign against the bosses been, that in 1900 he was nominated by acclamation and elected governor. As governor he fought for direct primary legislation, tax reform, and railroad control. At the Republican National Convention in Chicago in 1904 the La Follette delegates were unseated. This aroused in La Follette distrust of the progressivism of Theodore Roosevelt, who was nominated at that convention. After several terms as governor, La Follette was elected to the United States Senate in 1905, but did not take his seat or resign as governor until the next year, in order that he might finish his reform work in Wisconsin. Three times after 1905 La Follette was elected to succeed himself, and no abuse, ridicule, or organization on the part of his enemies could defeat him at the polls.

La Follette was a great friend and supporter of the University of Wisconsin, and much of its world-wide prominence and influence today is due to his ambitions

ROBERT M. LA FOLLETTE

for the University and the legislation which he fostered. He will long be remembered by those who were students at the University of Wisconsin during the years he was making his campaign for the governorship. To multitudes of undergraduates La Follette's name was like an army with banners. He took a friendly and personal interest in the students, especially in orators and debaters, and on occasions would leave important political conferences and law cases and go down to the court room of the old Dane County Court House and listen to the youthful orators as they delivered their speeches.[1]

John Bascom, one time president of the University of Wisconsin, and teacher of philosophy at Williams College, on a visit to La Follette after he became governor said to him, 'Robert, you will doubtless make mistakes of judgment as governor, but never mind the political mistakes, so long as you make no ethical mistakes." None ever charged La Follette's administration with ethical mistakes.

La Follette's name was first presented as a presidential candidate at the Republican National Convention of 1908, when Taft, at the insistence of Roosevelt, was nominated. He was again a candidate in 1912 and made an energetic campaign for the nomination. In his speeches he attacked great business and took the view that Socialism was inevitable unless the selfish tendencies of wealth were restrained. In this respect, his position was much the same as that of Franklin D. Roosevelt twenty years later. To help him in his campaigns, La Follette founded *La Follette's Weekly Magazine,* which with its caption from St. John's Gospel, "Ye shall know the truth and the truth shall make you free," had a wide circulation.

---

[1] Among them, the author of this book.

Those who heard La Follette speak in the spring of 1912, when he was seeking the support of delegates to the National Convention, will remember how optimistic he was with regard to the possibility of securing the nomination. There was a bitter revolt against Taft, and no other Progressive leader of the stature of La Follette had yet appeared on the scene.

During this campaign of 1912, La Follette had an unfortunate breakdown in Philadelphia at a dinner of the Periodical Publishers of the country. The speakers were the distinguished author and nerve specialist, Dr. S. Weir Mitchell, Woodrow Wilson, then governor of New Jersey, and La Follette. After Mitchell had spoken, Woodrow Wilson delivered one of his impressive speeches. When La Follette was introduced, he first bowed profusely to Wilson and uttered a sentence of salutation that sounded like a mocking defiance. Then, producing a thick manuscript, he began to read his speech, introducing it by saying he was going to tell the true story of money. With that he launched forth on a fierce attack on the journalists whose guest he was. As some of the diners began to leave in order to catch their trains for the suburbs, La Follette shook his fist at them and denounced them. For this he was called to order by the chairman. As he went along, shuffling the pages of his manuscript, but not laying them down, the amazed company at the banquet saw that he was repeating whole passages of his speech. He spoke from 10 to 11:30, when the hall was half empty, and continued his speech until 12:30, when he sank forward exhausted on the table. This breakdown, due to illness in his family and the physical strain of his campaign, was a most unfortunate incident, and from that time on La Follette was dropped from the consideration of many who had thought of him as a Progressive candidate to succeed Taft, but who now turned to Theodore Roosevelt. La Follette had no confidence in Roosevelt as a liberal and refused to bolt with him. He was again named by his Wisconsin supporters at the 1912 Convention.

Speaking at Wilmington, Delaware, October, 1912, Woodrow Wilson, then governor of New Jersey, and the nominee of the Democratic party for the presidency, said of La Follette: "I have sometimes thought of Senator La Follette climbing the mountain of privilege . . . taunted, laughed at, called back, going steadfastly on and not allowing himself to be deflected for a single moment, for fear he also should hearken and lose all his power to serve the great interests to which he had devoted himself. I love these lonely figures climbing the ugly mountain of privilege. But they are not so lonely now. I am sorry for my own part that I did not come in when they were fewer. There was no credit to come in when I did. The whole nation had awakened."

When the World War broke out in 1914, La Follette took a hostile attitude towards Great Britain and her allies. Some think that the fact that Roosevelt was so ardent a supporter of the Allies' cause had something to do with the position La Follette took. He denounced the ever-strengthening feeling in the United States to enter the war as the result of a conspiracy of American bankers to protect their loans to the Allies. At first friendly to many of the policies of Wilson, he now attacked Wilson's displomacy, did what he could to prevent legislation dealing with armed merchant ships, and voted against the declaration of war against Germany. In September, 1917, La Follette, by this time everywhere savagely denounced, and condemned even by the Wisconsin Legislature and the University of Wisconsin, was the object of an unsuccessful conspiracy to expel him from the Senate.

A misquotation by the press of the country of a speech delivered by La Follette in St. Paul, in which he was made to say that we had no grievance in the sinking of the *Lusitania*, aroused fierce resentment against him. When almost alone, and avoided by his old friends after he had voted against the entry of the United States into the war, La Follette said to a friend: "May I say to you that in the midst of this raging storm of hate, I am withal very happy. Insofar as my own future is concerned, I would not change places with any living man on the record as it stands today."

In spite of the position he had taken concerning the World War, and the charge that he was pro-German, La Follette was triumphantly reëlected in 1922. He fought Wilson on the ratification of the Covenant of the League of Nations, and when Coolidge was president was author of the resolution which brought about the investigation of the Teapot Dome leases, an investigation which had loud reverberation in Republican circles.

In 1924 a Progressive Republican Convention meeting at Cleveland nominated La Follette on an independent ticket. His running mate was the Democratic Senator from Montana, Burton K. Wheeler, who had carried on the investigation about the naval oil leases which La Follette had inaugurated. La Follette made a vigorous campaign, and there was some hope among his followers that he might be able to get sufficient votes to throw the election into the House of Representatives, where the Insurgents and Progressives might determine the choice. Almost five million voters stood by him at the polls.

This was La Follette's last battle. For many years he had waged his warfare with a thorn in his flesh and had survived serious operations; but now his vital energy was spent. He died June 18, 1925, and his mantle fell upon two able sons, Robert M. La Follette, Jr., now Senator from Wisconsin, and Philip La Follette, several times governor of Wisconsin. Those 4,800,000 votes in the election of 1924 represent the greatest personal tribute ever given to an American politician.

When he lay dying in 1925, La Follette said to his son Robert, the present Senator from Wisconsin: "I don't know how the people will feel towards me; but I will take to my grave my love for them, which has sustained me through life." There was no doubt about that. La Follette loved the people.

XIII

WILLIAM JENNINGS BRYAN

William Jennings Bryan ran three times for the presidency and missed it. But through the popularity, prestige and influence which came to him through those three campaigns for the presidency he was able to make another man president. Had it not been for Bryan, Woodrow Wilson would never have been president of the United States.

Bryan was not the only man who, defeated in his own aspirations for the presidency, was nevertheless able to promote another man to that high office. Clay was defeated in the election of 1824 when he ran against Jackson, Calhoun, and Crawford; but when the election was thrown into the House of Representatives, it was the vote and influence of Clay that made John Quincy Adams president. James G. Blaine was defeated for the nomination in 1876, again in 1880, and defeated as the Republican candidate in 1884. Yet it was his influence that made Garfield the successful candidate in 1880 and Harrison in 1888. Unable to attain to the presidency themselves, these men perhaps derived some consolation from the fact that they were strong enough to make another man president.

Bryan and Henry Clay are the only men in the history of the country who ran three times for the presidency, and every time he ran Bryan polled an enormous vote, more than six million. Had he been willing to do so, he could have been the candidate against Theodore

Roosevelt in 1904, but that year he refused to let his name go before the Convention, evidently feeling that Roosevelt could not be beaten. For undiminished popularity and unbroken hold upon his party, there is nothing comparable to the political history of Mr. Bryan.

Bryan was born March 4, 1860, at Salem, Illinois, the son of Judge Silas Bryan. Brought up in a godly home, Bryan was converted at the age of fourteen and united with the Presbyterian Church. He always referred to this as the most important event in his life. No analysis of Bryan's character and career is adequate which leaves out that deep conviction. Bryan graduated with honors at Illinois College, Jacksonville, Illinois, studied in the law office of Lyman Trumbull at Chicago, and practiced law for three years with modest success at Jacksonville. In 1887 he removed to Lincoln, Nebraska, where in his first months of practice he slept on a lounge in his office and lived on two meals a day. He took an active part in politics, became popular as a Fourth of July and Chautauqua orator, served two terms in Congress, and was the editor of the *Omaha World Herald*.

When the Democratic Convention met in Chicago in 1896, Bryan was an enthusiastic advocate of the Free Silver cause. The nationally known leader, however, was Richard Bland of Missouri, who was most spoken of for the nomination. But a series of fortunate events pushed Bryan to the front. He was asked by the Silver men to take charge of the debate on the Silver Plank before the Convention. Senator Ben Tillman of South Carolina was to close the debate with a fifty-minute speech. But this was regarded as too long a speech, and it was arranged instead that Tillman should open the debate and Bryan close it. After the Gold Democrats, able men like Senator Hill of New York, Vilas of Wisconsin, and Russell of Massachusetts, had spoken for their side, Bryan took the platform and was given an enthusiastic ovation by the Silver men in the Convention.

Never was there such a Convention speech and never such a demonstration. After a happy introduction, and with his powerful and resonant voice reaching to the remotest parts of the Coliseum, Bryan had the rapt attention of the delegates. Speaking of that memorable occasion, Bryan said: "The audience seemed to rise and sit down as one man. At the close of a sentence it would rise and shout, and when I began upon another sentence the room was as still as a church. The audience acted like a trained choir."

Bryan made the Convention roar when he referred to the fact that Major McKinley, the Republican nominee, and who was said to look like Napoleon, was nominated on the anniversary of the Battle of Waterloo. By and by came this stirring challenge: "We have petitioned, and our petitions have been scorned. We have entreated, and our entreaties have been disregarded. We have begged, and they have mocked when our calamity came. We beg no longer! We entreat no more! We petition no more! We defy them!" Then came the famous peroration: "Having behind us the producing masses of this nation and of the world, supported by the commercial interests, the laboring interests and toilers everywhere, we will answer their demand for a gold standard by saying to them, 'You shall not press down upon the brow of labor this crown of thorns. You shall not crucify mankind upon a cross of gold.'"

WILLIAM JENNINGS BRYAN

His speech was extemporaneous only with respect to the arrangement of its parts, for Bryan had been covering the subject in its every aspect in his addresses during the past few years. Even the famous "crown of thorns and cross of gold" peroration had been used several times before and "laid away," he said, "for the proper occasion." Twenty-eight years afterwards, a friend of Bryan, driving with him in a taxicab, passed the Coliseum. His friend [1] said to Bryan, "Mr. Bryan, I suppose that often before you had made just as able a speech as that speech at the Convention, and it was never heard of?" "Yes," responded Bryan, "but that Convention was my opportunity and I made the most of it." Then, after a moment's silence, he added, as the light of recollection came into his great eyes, "And that's about all we do in this life—use or lose our opportunity."

In the extraordinary campaign that followed, Bryan toured the country, speaking to immense audiences. Covered with abuse and ridicule, he kept his balance, and during his swing around the circle of 18,000 miles carried his ideas home to the people as no man had ever done since the days of Henry Clay. Had the election been held in midsummer or in September, Bryan would probably have been elected. He polled only 606,000 less votes than McKinley and had 176 electoral votes.

When the Spanish War broke out Bryan was made a colonel in the Volunteers, but gave up his commission the moment the treaty of peace was signed. In 1900 he was again a candidate and took for his issue, "Anti-Imperialism," although it was his personal influence with Democratic Senators which had brought about the

---

[1] Clarence Edward Macartney.

ratification of the annexation of the Philippines. He refused to be a candidate in 1904. In 1908 he was again the Democratic nominee, but was defeated by Taft.

It was in the Democratic Convention of 1912 that Bryan played one of the most powerful and dramatic parts in the history of American politics. The leading candidates for the nomination were Champ Clark of Missouri and Woodrow Wilson of New Jersey. The Nebraska delegation, of which Bryan was a member, were instructed to vote for Clark. Bryan undoubtedly preferred Wilson to Clark, but for thirteen ballots he voted for Clark. At the very opening of the Convention Bryan introduced a motion that the Convention "declare ourselves opposed to the nomination of any candidate for president who is the representative of, or under obligation to, J. Pierpont Morgan, Thomas F. Ryan, August Belmont, or any other member of the privilege company and favor-seeking classes." This extraordinary resolution was passed by a vote of 899 to 196, and showed the power of Bryan in the Convention. The Wilson delegates nearly all voted for the Resolution, but nearly all the Clark delegates voted against it.

When the Convention proceeded to vote on the candidates, Clark led Wilson by more than a hundred votes, but was considerably short of the 725 necessary to nominate. On the tenth ballot the New York delegation switched from Harmon, of Ohio, for whom it had been voting, to Clark. In the Resolutions Committee room Bryan heard the uproar and hurried to the floor and took his seat with the Nebraska delegation, and never left the hall during the sessions of the Convention. A sergeant-at-arms supplied him with water and his brother Charles supplied him with sandwiches. Bryan voted for Clark through the thirteenth ballot, although some of his delegation had already turned to Wilson. On the thirteenth ballot the vote stood, Clark 556, Wilson 340. Senator W. J. Stone, of Missouri, Clark's manager, telephoned to Wilson at Spring Lake, New Jersey, the summer headquarters of the governor, that he ought not to delay the nomination of Clark, which was desired by the majority of the delegates. Wilson then telephoned to his floor manager, William J. McCombs, saying: "Stone's logic is correct," and authorized McCombs to withdraw his name if he thought best. He actually sat down to write a telegram of congratulation to Clark; but his friends persuaded him to withhold it.

On the fourteenth ballot, when Nebraska was called its chairman cast its vote for Clark again. One of the delegates, however, demanded that the delegation be polled. When Bryan's name was called, he arose to explain his vote. The delegates shouted: "Regular order!" The permanent chairman, William Sulzer, Congressman from New York, and afterwards its ill-starred governor, said: "Under the rules, nothing is in order but the completion of the roll. How does the gentleman vote?" Bryan then answered: "As long as Mr. Ryan's—as long as New York's 90 votes are recorded for Mr. Clark, I withdraw my vote to cast it for Nebraska's second choice, Governor Wilson."

The greatest disorder and excitement then ensued, for the whole convention seemed to sense that Clark was doomed. Bryan was still making an effort amid shouts, jeers and cheers to get to the platform. Clark's manager, Senator Stone, sure that nothing now could stop Clark, and thinking to be generous toward Bryan, moved unanimous consent for Bryan to explain his vote. Bryan, although out of order, then took the plat form, and in a stirring address denounced August Belmont, J. P. Morgan, Thomas F. Ryan and Tammany Hall. "No man," he shouted, "should be nominated to whom, if elected, the money trust could say 'Remember now, thy creator.' "

In the excitement which swept the convention after Bryan's speech, Chairman Sulzer rushed over to Charles F. Murphy, of Tammany Hall, and exclaimed: "I can be nominated, if New York will stand by me!"

Clark supporters paraded through the hall with a great banner on which was inscribed the sentence Bryan had used in eulogizing Clark in 1910. When Bryan was trying to get the floor to explain the time and the conditions under which he had spoken this eulogy, he was threatened by Clark supporters. He said it was the only time in his life when he was in danger of physical harm.

As the balloting continued, Clark issued a statement in which he denounced Bryan's insinuations as false and infamous and denied that he would be under the control of Wall Street. But Bryan's speech and change of vote were the end of Clark. On the forty-sixth ballot Wilson was nominated. This was the most remarkable triumph in Bryan's long political career. It was all the more remarkable in that some time before the Convention a letter had been made public in which Wilson had said to a friend that he hoped Bryan would be "knocked into a cocked hat." A man of smaller caliber than Bryan would not have forgotten that letter.

There were many delegates in the Convention who favored Bryan. Some held the view that Bryan was trying to deadlock the Convention in order that he might secure the nomination himself. But he refused to yield to the plea of his friends in the Convention that he permit his name to go before the Convention, and in so doing scored his most notable triumph.

Like other defeated candidates for the presidency, Clay, Seward, and Webster, Bryan was made Secretary of State. Much of the reform legislation passed in President Wilson's first term was carried through Congress through the influence of Bryan. In 1915, after the sinking of the *Lusitania,* Bryan, rather than despatch the note which President Wilson had drafted to Germany, resigned his post, knowing well the storm of ridicule and abuse which would burst upon him. This was perhaps the most courageous act in his history. Today, in the midst of another world war, the national sentiment is so different from what it was in 1915, that a man who took Bryan's course and resigned from the Cabinet for the reasons he did, would be praised rather than condemned.

Bryan's last appearance at a political Convention was in 1924, when amid the insults of the rabble which filled the galleries, he opposed the nomination of Governor Alfred E. Smith and defeated the resolution of denunciation which named the Ku Klux Klan. It was at a meeting of the platform committee that, after Judge McCann, a Catholic from Pennsylvania, had recited the Lord's Prayer, Mr. Bryan made a fervent extemporary prayer asking for Divine guidance. This was at six o'clock in the morning and the newspaper spoke of it as the "Daybreak Prayer." But no one charged Bryan with cant or hypocrisy. Few men in public life could have done as naturally and as easily what Bryan did at the meeting of that committee.

During all the years which had elapsed since his first nomination at Chicago, the Great Commoner waged a campaign among the people of the land for temperance, righteousness, and peace. His most popular lecture was *"The Prince of Peace,"* not, however, an advocacy of peace, but a defense of the Christian Faith. His last years were devoted to an earnest attack upon the evolutionary hypothesis, which he believed was doing a great injury to the Church and to the nation. His last public appearance was as an assistant to the prosecutor in the trial of a teacher at Dayton, Tennessee, for the violation of the Tennessee Statute forbidding the teaching of any theory which denied the Divine creation of man as taught in the Bible. Bryan's contention that the teaching of the evolutionary hypothesis was hostile to religion was, in a way, strikingly upheld by the appearance at the trial as counsel for defense of noted agnostics and atheists, such as Clarence Darrow. A few days after the conviction of Scopes, the Great Commoner died in his sleep, July 26, 1925, at Dayton ,Tennessee. Although he had been the great advocate of peace, and as Secretary of State the signer of many peace treaties, he was buried at his own request in Arlington Cemetery, where soldiers and generals await the trumpet of the Resurrection.

Denounced as a dreamer and a fanatic, Bryan lived to see many of the measures he had advocated enacted into law. Among these were woman suffrage, the popular election of Senators, prohibition, labor representation in the Cabinet, and currency reform.

Bryan was a man of noble appearance. His frame was stalwart and his figure, until near the end of his life, strong and upright. His voice was one that could never be forgotten, melodious and friendly in familiar conversation, and at other times ringing out like a silver trumpet. He was a man of great humility, and

his national popularity and influence never separated
him from the common people.

He had a keen sense of humor. On the wall of the
library of his Florida home he displayed many of the
cartoons of himself which had appeared in the newspapers during his three campaigns. He had an ample
mouth, and the cartoon which pleased him most of all
was one which depicted him as whispering in his own
ear. He was not a great reader, but the greatest of all
books he knew thoroughly. Referring to his three de-
feats for the presidency, he would sometimes tell the
story of a drunken man, who, when he had been thrown
down the stairs of a dance hall for the third time, gathered himself up and said, "Those fellows can't fool me.
They don't want me in there, and they think I don't
know it."

XIV

CHARLES EVANS HUGHES

At ten-thirty on the night of November 7, 1916, I stood on Broad Street, Philadelphia, and watched a jubilant and excited crowd of bankers and business men pour down the steps of the Union League, the Republican citadel of that city, and stage an impromptu parade down the street. The hated Wilson had been defeated; Hughes was elected; the Democrats were out; the Republicans, alone fit to rule the country, were in again. Similar demonstrations and parades took place all over the country. But by the next night it was the Democrats, and not the Republicans, who were shouting and parading down the avenues.

Charles Evans Hughes was one of the two candidates for the presidency who had the bitter experience of feeling sure on the night of the election, and on the morning following, that they had been elected, only to learn later that they had lost. The other was Tilden; but with this difference, that whereas there was no doubt as to the defeat of Hughes, Tilden and his supporters never acknowledged defeat. But both men knew the bitterness of defeat after being hailed as the next president.

No candidate was ever better fitted for the presidency than Hughes, and if he had stayed out of California on his swing around the circle in the 1916 campaign, undoubtedly he would have won the great prize.

When Hughes was nominated by the 1916 Republican Convention, he appeared to have everything that a successful candidate for the presidency ought to have. He sprang from the best middle class of the nation; he was the son of a minister; was well educated, of superior intellect; an experienced and successful executive of the nation's greatest state; had a record of notable reforms as governor of New York; looked the great man; had been a strong campaigner in two New York elections, and his name was a synonym of personal integrity and righteousness.

Charles Evans Hughes was born at Glen Falls, N. Y., April 11, 1862, the son, and only child, of a Baptist preacher, David Charles Hughes. Both father and mother were well educated, and Hughes' superior education commenced in his own home, a home of plain living and high thinking. After preliminary schooling in Oswego and in Newark, N. J., where his father held pastorates, he spent a year at Colgate University, and then entered Brown University, where he was graduated with the highest honors. He taught the classics for a time at the Delaware Academy at Delhi, New York, and then entered the law school of Columbia University.

In 1888, at the age of twenty-six, he became a member of the law firm of Carter, Hughes and Cravath, soon after marrying the daughter of the head of the firm. In 1891, he was made professor of law in the law school of Cornell University, but soon returned to the active practice in the firm of his father-in-law.

In a few years his abilities were so marked and recognized that he was appointed to head the investigation of the insurance companies of New York. He carried out this investigation with indefatigable industry, great resourcefulness and undismayed courage. When his enemies, in order to discredit him and the investigation, had published in certain newspapers bogus accounts of the investigation, Hughes summoned the publishers and editors of the newspapers to the witness stand and exposed the conspiracy. The insurance investigation made Hughes a national figure, just as Thomas Dewey's successful prosecution of prominent Tammany politicians has made him a national figure and a contender for the presidential nomination. Elected as governor of New York in 1906, Hughes carried out important reforms, such as the public utilities commissions, primary elections, and the anti-racetrack gambling law. This made him anathema to certain elements in New York, who dubbed him, "Charles the Baptist," but enhanced his popularity in the country at large.

In 1908 he was reelected governor of New York, defeating William R. Hearst, who if he had been successful in that election, would have been a serious contender for the next Democratic presidential nomination. It was in this campaign that Hughes exposed Hearst's method of evading responsibility and legal judgments by organizing one company within another. This resulted in the law requiring newspapers to publish the name of their responsible owners and editors.

New York favored Hughes for the Republican presidential nomination in 1908; but a coolness had arisen between Roosevelt and Hughes because of the latter's disregard of a request of Roosevelt with regard to some measure pending in the New York legislature. Roosevelt, who was able to name his successor, preferred Taft to Hughes, and the proconsul of the Philippines was nominated and elected.

In May, 1910, Hughes startled the country, and shocked many of his friends and supporters, by resigning the governorship of New York and accepting a seat

on the Supreme Court of the United States, to which
he had been named by President Taft.   Many who had
thrilled to the leadership of Hughes as a political reformer felt that he had deserted the cause.   Hughes
declared he was weary after three years of incessant
battling in New York, and welcomed the quietude of the
Supreme Court.   Probably he thought, as Chief Justice
Chase had thought when Lincoln named him to Taney's
post, that he would be more happy and contented there
than anywhere else.   But just as Chase's political aspirations did not die with his appointment to the Supreme
Court, neither did those of Hughes.

As the country began to look forward to the 1916
campaign, there arose a strong demand that Hughes be
the leader of the Republican cause.   The party had
been rent in twain by the strife of 1912 when Theodore
Roosevelt headed a third party, the Progressive, or Bull
Moose, party.   The wounds of that conflict were not
yet sufficiently healed to permit the nomination of
Roosevelt, and more and more the rank and file of the
party began to think of Hughes as the only man who
could defeat Wilson.

Hughes was nominated on the third ballot at the convention meeting in the Coliseum, Chicago, with Fairbanks of Indiana, and vice-president with Roosevelt, as
his running mate.   Fairbanks was spoken of as "the
man who had never offended anybody."   Two minutes
before the Republican nomination, the Progressives,
meeting in the Chicago Auditorium, nominated Roosevelt.   He withheld his acceptance of the nomination for
a time, and then definitely rejected it.

This was the end of the Progressive Party.   A cartoon of the day shows Roosevelt in Rough Rider uni-
form putting a pistol to the head of a dejected moose,

with the caption, "This hurts me worse than it hurts you." The meeting of the Progressive Convention, however, made it necessary for the regular Republicans to nominate a man of the type of Hughes, and the rejection of the Progressive nomination by Roosevelt gave Hughes his splendid chance for election, for had Roosevelt headed a third ticket, the election of Wilson would have been assured, as it was in 1912, when Wilson, Taft and Roosevelt were the candidates.

The campaign of the two preachers' sons, Baptist and Presbyterian, promised to be one of great interest. The Republicans now had a candidate whose record for reform was as good as Wilson's, whose education was as thorough and whose intellect was as superior. Moreover, Hughes, like Wilson in 1912, was the choice, not of the politician and machine bosses, but of the people and the rank and file of his party. Yet the hopes of the Republicans were disappointed, for it was in spite of the campaign Hughes made, and not because of it, that he was almost elected.

Since Hughes had been for six years on the Supreme Court, and removed from popular politics and discussions, and had gained a certain reputation for coldness and aloofness, the Republican managers decided to send him on a great "swing around the country" while Wilson remained at Shadow Lawn, New Jersey, occasionally making one of his telling speeches.

Hughes was sensitive to this reputation for coldness and lack of humanity, and once remarked, "If they perform an autopsy on me, I hope they will find something besides sawdust and briefs inside." Yet, in spite of his "swing around the circle" and his efforts to show that he was human and affable, such as at a ball game in Detroit leaping from the railing after the game to the concrete roof of the Tigers' dugout and shaking hands with the members of both teams and chatting for a time with Ty Cobb, Hughes was never able to make the common people warm up to him. I heard him speak at a great meeting in Philadelphia. He looked the great man, the man of high character and spoke as a man of high ability, yet there was nothing in his manner or speech which was of a nature to woo the voter.

As the campaign went on, Hughes greatly disappointed his supporters on the intellectual side also. Something seemed to have happened to that fine mind and that lofty spirit, once flaming with moral passion and righteousness. His speeches never rose to the high level of Wilson's. In October, the Nation, which had been his ardent supporter, said, 'The failure of Hughes is indeed something like a calamity."

Yet, in spite of Hughes' amazing failure as a campaigner, it looked as if he would be elected, so strong was the tide running against Wilson and his policies. The issues discussed in the campaign were Woman Suffrage, endorsed by both parties, protective tariff, the administration's policy in Mexico, railroad labor laws, and, as the first World War was then raging, preparedness, and the foreign policy of the United States. The slogan of the Democrats, and one of the best ever coined, was, "He kept us out of war."

Wilson's courageous and scathing rebuke of a New York Democrat, Jeremiah O'Leary, who had heckled him on the Irish question, alienated many Irish voters in New York City, and the chances looked good for Hughes to carry the Empire State, which, indeed, he did. Had he remained away from California, he would have been elected.

The Republican party in California had two factions, the Progressive element, headed by Hiram Johnson, then Governor of the state, and the Old Guard Republicans who hated Johnson and all his works. As the campaign proceeded, members of the Republican National Committee became anxious as to the way things were being handled in California, and telegrams were exchanged with the Old Guard leaders, who assured the Committee that all would be well.

When Hughes entered the state he was immediately taken in tow by the Republican Bourbons and foes of Johnson, such as William H. Crocker and H. G. Otis, the editor of the *Los Angeles Times*. Johnson never appeared at the meetings at which Hughes spoke and the two men never shook hands. Some said that Johnson kept himself out of the way of Hughes; but the two men never met. The extraordinary thing was that Hughes, so experienced a campaigner, permitted himself to be put in such a dangerous situation. During the campaign, Johnson, who had won the Republican senatorial nomination by an enormous majority, spoke, and with apparent sincerity, for Hughes, praised his record, and asked his own followers to support Hughes. How they answered his appeal, the election showed. Johnson was elected senator by a plurality of 300,000, while Hughes lost the state, and the presidency, by 3,000 votes.

At ten-thirty on the night of the election, Fairbanks, Hughes' running mate, sent him a telegram of congratulation. This was one of thousands that poured in upon him. The Republicans had carried the great, and then doubtful, states of New York, Indiana, and Illinois. Only two northern states, east of the Great Divide, Minnesota and Ohio, had gone for Wilson. No wonder the Republicans cheered and staged hilarious parades and celebrations. But they had forgotten the west.

Hughes went to bed on the night of the 7th of November, 1916, confident that he had been elected president of the United States. But the far western states, and, above all, California, were still to be heard from. The final count showed that Hughes had lost the state by three thousand votes. The thirteen California votes gave Wilson 276 electoral votes to 255 for Hughes. The Republican parades broke up in gloom. Hughes was beaten. Wilson was reelected.

In an early edition on the 8th of November the New York *World* displayed a cartoon by Cassel, which showed Hughes in shirt sleves sitting at the presidential desk in the White House, with Uncle Sam standing behind his chair with a hand of encouragement laid on Hughes' shoulder. Underneath was the caption, "A New Man on the Job." But the next edition of the *World,* with the same general setting, had Wilson in shirt sleves in the presidential chair, with Uncle Sam standing behind him, and the caption, "Keep right on the job."

In 1921 Hughes accepted the chief place in the cabinet of the weakest and least worthy of all our presidents, Harding, and there, as Secretary of State, this former Justice of the Supreme Court sat in the company of such men as Daugherty and the ignoble Fall. In the Washington Conference Hughes took the brilliant lead in the international agreements which bound the nations to tear up blue prints and sink battleships.

President Hoover named Hughes as Chief Justice of the Supreme Court in 1929, succeeding the late Chief Justice and former president, William H. Taft. Thus

Hughes became the leader of the "nine old men" whom Franklin D. Roosevelt charged with obstructing progressive and liberal legislation.

As he sits there in his black robe, presiding over that august Court as the interpreter of the laws of the land, does the mind of Chief Justice Hughes sometimes run back to that November night in 1916, when he, like thousands of others, was sure that he had been elected the nation's Chief Executive?